THE 7 LEVELS OF CHANGE

THE 7 LEVELS OF CHANGE

The Guide to Innovation in the World's Largest Corporations

By Rolf Smith

THE SUMMIT PUBLISHING GROUP
One Arlington Centre, 1112 East Copeland Road, Fifth Floor
Arlington, Texas 76011
summit@dfw.net
www.summitbooks.com

Printed in the United States of America.
01 00 99 98 97   010   5 4 3 2 1

Library of Congress Cataloging-in-Publication Data

Smith, Rolf, 1940-
    The 7 levels of change : the guide to innovation in the world's largest corportions
/ by Rolf Smith.
        p.   cm.
    Includes bibliographical references.
    ISBN 1-56530-207-9
    1. Organizational change.   I. Title.   II. Title: Seven levels of change.
HD58.8.S638 1997
658.4'06—dc21
                                                                96-51302
                                                                CIP

Cover design by Dennis Davidson
Book design by Michael Melton

DEDICATION

LEVEL 1
Effectiveness—Doing the right things
To Al Lewis who kept saying, "You've got to write a book."

LEVEL 2
Efficiency—Doing the right things right
To Tom Martinez who kept asking, "When are you going to
work on the book?"

LEVEL 3
Improving—Doing things better
To Mike Donahue who kept saying, "That's a great story!
You've got to put that in your book."

LEVEL 4
Cutting—Doing away with things
To Peter Hearl who kept telling me, "Rolf, you're crazy!
You've got to take that out of your book."

LEVEL 5
Copying—Doing things other people are doing
To Dale Clauson who kept warning me, "You're going to jail.
You copied that."

LEVEL 6
Different—Doing things no one else is doing
To my sister, Bozier Demaree, who has asked me all my life,
"When will I see your book in a bookstore?"

LEVEL 7
Impossible—Doing things that can't be done
To my wife, Juliane, who kept pointing out, "You're never
going to write a book if you don't write it."

LEVEL 8
Beyond Impossible
To Sally Giddens Stephenson who said, "It's done."

CONTENTS

ACKNOWLEDGMENTS ix

Putting this book together was a Level 7 experience. It brought home to me personally an idea I've been talking about for a long time: It's not the summit, it's the climb that makes the expedition. That and getting back alive. Feel the fear and do it anyway.

Thanks to my family for putting up with it. They were on a lot of this expedition with me. They all helped tremendously, frequently even listening to my ideas. "Not all ideas are good ideas," they'd throw back at me. "Keep trying, one of these times you'll have a good idea," was my wife Julie's favorite retort. And she did more than her fair share of idea finding and editing while I was looking for a good idea.

I had a lot of different kinds of special help from good friends, and some of them often didn't even realize it: Boaz Arch, Al Lewis, Eileen Ong, Bobby Wadsworth, Scott Swanson, Mike Donahue, Randy Randol, George Abide, Nadir Muwwakkil, Dake Rohe, my Dad—Gerry Eckstein, Ron Bowen, Matt Hoffner, George Gammon, Tom Martinez, Paul Krause, Bill Olsen, Stan Gryskiewicz, Chuck Grey, Mary Wallgren, Bill Keeter, Sherman Glass, Mike Brezina, David Tanner, J. B. Groves, Matt Hoffner, Ed Varian, Lynn Lee, Henry Osti, and Bill Olsen.

Joe Miguez and my son, Rolf, gave me a lot of ideas for the Mindmapping.

Robin Dalred and OPTIMA Image brought some amazing talent to bear in developing and evolving the 35mm slides and artwork that really made the 7 Levels of Change come together visually in workshops and on Thinking Expeditions.

Dale Clauson, my partner, put up with me and ran a lot of interference so I could check out and get some thinking and writing done. And together we came up with one really great Myers Briggs insight in the process.

The Houston Executive Club played into and tested a lot of my ideas. When Bob Holloway, a longtime member,

NOTE: I've used copies of the slides to create a "slide show" on the pages of this book.

X

realized I really did want to write a book, he made the initial connection for me with the Summit Publishing Group. Later, he and I got on an airplane and flew to Fort Worth to make the book happen.

Going on a yearlong Thinking Expedition® with the Summit Publishing Group was a full-blown, 7-Level experience for all of us. My teammates, Len Oszustowicz, Mark Murphy, David Gavin, Brent Lockhart, Sally Giddens Stephenson, and I hit some big crevasses and unexpected avalanches along the route and changed course several times. A couple of times we had to send out search parties. Mark operated as our base camp manager and senior editor, and Len, my publisher, kept his eye on the weather and timelines. When we got ready for the summit attempt, things were pretty tense.

"Where did this start?" was a question I found myself often reflecting on. Back in 1989, while I was working with Exxon in the Innovations Group in Marketing, Don Taylor, the group coordinator, said: "We need to figure out a way to connect continuous improvement and innovation." To the best of my recollection, that's when I started playing around with the idea of levels, first as levels of innovation—and I started feeling out the concept with the Innovation and Continuous Improvement workshops we were running all over Exxon. Don had pushed me into coming up with something that looked . . . interesting. Later, Dick Reid and, especially, George Saltsman were a big influence on my moving toward seeing the concept as powerful as it became.

I've used the Association of Managers of Innovation (AMI) for sanity checks and ideas for a long time. AMI is a loosely coupled group of Fortune 500 thinkers and leaders who are making innovation happen in their organizations. In the spring of 1989, I tried out the Levels of Innovation concept on them. I took away some great observations and suggestions that led me into looking at the ideas and the sizes of change behind innovations and ultimately at scale.

Michael Kirton's Adaption-Innovation theory and his KAI Inventory have been invaluable to me right from the start, clarifying the idea of relative change and differing perspectives and helping me help people understand change differently.

Ray Slesenski and I teamed up and wrote the first article on the 7 Levels of Change for Stephen Covey's *Executive Excellence* magazine in May 1991. Ray convinced me to buy a fax machine so we could ping-pong our draft copies and changes back and forth more easily. Writing that article with Ray really clarified my thinking on the distinctiveness of each of the levels, and the fax machine changed my life.

Sparked by DuPont and a major meeting at which I had been invited to speak, Al Lewis, Jim Brown, Ray Slesenski, and I spent a late evening in the Exxon Innovation Center brainstorming the 7 Levels of Change for Work & Home. More importantly, we developed the ideas into a yellow card with the 7 Levels on each side of it that we still use today. It was designed to go on a refrigerator door—and I actually got a number of letters about it from attendees at the DuPont meeting.

Every School for Innovators has been an operational research and development cauldron for the 7 Levels of Change. School XVIII was probably the first one in which the 7 Levels had an integral part, and from then on the model was a mainstay in one form or another. I owe many, many thank-yous to all the graduates—they served as an operational test bed for the 7 Levels of Change concepts. Five of the Schools for Innovators in particular, which were sponsored primarily by single companies, allowed us to explore a variety of ways to apply the concept of the 7 Levels as a creative problem-solving tool and develop supporting processes and techniques for the model. The sponsoring companies were: IBM (1991), Hoechst Celanese (1993), KFC Australia and New Zealand (1991, 1992, and 1993), and Johnson & Johnson (1995). Gene Quidort, John Mozeliak, Tom Wojcik, Ray Kilminster, Bruce Wright, Peter Hearl, Barbara Elbertson, and Gerry Kells were the sponsors and backers.

Hoechst Celanese Corporation sent Randy McSwain to our first School for Innovators (1991) that connected rock climbing and expeditionary thinking to the 7 Levels of Change. And Randy in turn came up with the basics for the Mindshift Model—thinking about thinking—that underlies the thinking connected with each level of change.

Tip! A copy of the card is in the back of the book. Cut it out, carry it with you

The MINDSHIFT MODEL

xii

Thinking Expeditions in Schools? See case study on Campbell Junior High!

Gwen Keith, principal of Campbell Junior High School in Houston's Cypress Fairbanks Independent School District, has taken everything she learned in the School for Innovators and is turning Campbell into an expedition school. Her assistant principal, director of curriculum, and two of her teachers are School for Innovators graduates—and she has created a Thinking Expedition track for one quarter of the school. She has used the 7 Levels mindshift model continuously and keeps giving me new insights and ideas on how to refine it further.

A number of companies have invited me to come in and talk specifically about the 7 Levels of Change at meetings and conferences: Exxon, of course, companywide (1988–1992); IBM, through John Barnshaw (1992); the DuPont OZ Group twice, initially in 1991; R. J. Reynolds BIG BANG (1993); Hoechst Celanese (1992–1994); Texaco (1994); Army Air Force Exchange Service Television (1995); Proctor & Gamble (1995–1996); General Mills (1994–1996); Fletcher Challenge in New Zealand (1996); Cadillac Fairview in Canada (1996); the U.S. Navy SMART SHIP Team (1995–1996). Every one of these companies added breadth and depth to my own understanding of the 7 Levels of Change.

Each time I worked with large companies like these, three things happened: (1) While I was preparing, I made a lot of changes and updates to what I had presented or done the previous time; (2) I made the sessions heavily interactive, and, as a result, I got a lot of ideas and input on ways to make the 7 Levels connect with people even better; (3) In each of those companies, people really gave me some deep insights on the concept. Some of the people who played into and have influenced my thinking through those kinds of company-sponsored forums are: John Barnshaw, Steve Sheriff, Lynn Lee, David Tanner, George Pransky, Lynn DeLean, Tom McMullen, Ed Malerik, and Dorris Balsam.

For information on attending CPSI, call CEF 1-800-447-2774

The Creative Problem Solving Institute (CPSI–1994, 1995, and 1996) and the Creative Education Foundation (CEF) offered me some wonderful forums and test beds to develop the 7 Levels even further, as did the Small Business Administration's annual Creativity, Innovation, and

Entrepreneurship conferences. That's where I met Henry Osti and Joe Miguez.

We built the 7 Levels, Me, Inc.®, and the Mindshift Model heavily into R. J. Reynolds BIG BANG and Innovation Week. Major new connections came out of that operation for me. It was the forerunner of the Thinking Expeditions of today. Thanks to Harold Crayton Threatt, Carl Ehmann, Tom Perfetti, Alan Norman, Mike Dube, Jamie Chesterton, and Jim McPhail.

But in the end, it's been on Thinking Expeditions that I have gained the most insights and learned the most. Something about focusing on urgent Level 7 results while ootching through the other six levels brings clarity to the concept for me that nothing else does. Some of the expeditions where I personally got distinct mindshifts and breakthroughs in my own thinking were: Exxon, ARCO, and British Petroleum (Alaska, 1993); Exxon (Houston, 1994); BOC Gases (1995); WMX Technologies (1994); Battelle Northwest Laboratories (1995); General Mills (1995, 1996); Proctor & Gamble (1995, 1996); Honeywell (1996); Cadillac Fairview (Toronto, 1996); Fletcher Wood Panels (Auckland, New Zealand, 1996); U.S. Navy SMART SHIP (1995, 1996). I owe the Thinking Expedition leaders, backers, and sponsors a lot: Ron Bowen, Gary Roberts, Craig Parker, John Biedry, Nancy Kosciolek, Dave Ross, Mike Nelson, Jeff Bellaires, Mary Wallgren, Bill Keeter, Lynn Lee, Ted Reece, Mary Jane Grant, Scott Knaut, Peter Sharpe, Peter O'Sullivan, Tom Laughlin, Henry Osti, Colin Leach, Heike Schiele, and U.S. Navy Captains Tom Zysk, Grey Glover, and Jim Baskerville.

xiv

vTx – The Virtual Thinking Expedition Company

During most of the climbing and exploring on the Thinking Expedition that was the writing of this book, Sally Giddens Stephenson and I were running as a small rope team. I did the lead climbing, and Sally belayed me. We'd debrief each pitch and move on into a new route at the next level of change. I especially want to thank Sally for helping me capture my thinking in ways that made surprising sense to me. It was magic.

Only in the process of writing this book have I discovered just how much I personally live and move through the reference points of the 7 Levels of Change every day with vTx, our virtual Thinking Expedition company. Bill Olsen (Washington, D.C.), Boaz Arch (Houston), Dale Clauson (Houston), David Purkiss (Virginia Beach), Frank Luton (Atlanta), George Abide (Minneapolis), Joe Miguez (Boulder), Lynn Lee (Cincinnati), my son Rolf (San Antonio), and I are all roped together with E-mail into a virtual company. Who we are and what we do continuously changes with every Thinking Expedition we conceptualize and organize. When we clip out of our virtual company mode, link up physically with a team of clients at some off-site location, and go into actual execution, we're once again moving out into the unknown on a new adventure through the 7 Levels of Change.

One final acknowledgment: I'm not sure I fully understand everything I know about this.

Rolf Smith
Houston, Texas

HOW TO USE THIS BOOK

This book is diffferent. Unlike many works of fiction and nonfiction, you don't have to start at the beginning and read straight through to understand what's happening at each level of change—although there are some advantages to doing it that way. Reading from Level 1 to Level 7 helps to flatten out the rough spots between the mindshifts. The 7 Levels evolved into their sequence because the sequence works, yet the concepts aren't increasingly difficult as they progress through the levels. The changes they deal with, however, are typically more difficult to sell and to implement as they climb toward Level 7. Yet, you don't have to go through all of the lower levels of change to make a Level 7 change. That said, you may want to consider using the book in one of the following ways:

JUMP AROUND IN THE BOOK.

People are different and are looking for different things when they pick up a book. I had an idea when I decided to put together this book. You had another idea when you first picked up this book to look at it. It's very likely that those ideas are quite diffferent. The way you read this and the way I wrote it are not going to be the same. I have no idea in which direction your ideas will take my ideas. Your thinking shifts constantly, and an idea at one level will spark an idea at another.

The basic framework of the 7 Levels is almost intuitively simple. After you understand the concept and the relationship among the 7 Levels, it's easy to jump around. So, just read what you are interested in. Flip through to each level, read the brief overview that begins the discussion of that level, and omit the sections that don't immediately connect for you.

USE THE MINDMAPS.

There are eight Mindmaps in this book to help you find your way through the 7 Levels—one for the entire book at the end of the book, and one for each level of change. Mindmaps are a simple, fast, and efficient way of capturing ideas in chunks that are easy to look at, understand, and remember. The concept of Mindmapping originated with Tony Buzan, author of *Use Both Sides of Your Brain*, who developed the technique based on research that indicates the brain fundamentally works with key concepts in an interrelated and integrated way. Your brain doesn't create ideas and thoughts in a linear fashion. It jumps around. Mindmapping allows you to use your whole brain—both the creative and analytical sides—by freeing you from the constraints of linear thinking. It also gives you an immediate big picture of each chapter.

FLIP THROUGH THE SLIDE SHOW.

In the left page margins throughout the book are copies of the sequence of 35mm slides I've developed and used on Thinking Expeditions with some of the world's largest corporations to help them be more creative and innovative. (Thinking Expeditions are an accelerated change process during which a team is formed to attack an urgent and pressing problem, come to terms with change, or create change for revolutionary results.) The slides themselves present a good overview of the concepts in this book. By flipping the pages slowly with your thumb, you can visually move through the 7 Levels of Change at high speed. Try it!

Appendix III in the back of the book explains in more detail how you can create an exciting 7 Levels of Change slide presentation and workshop by dropping personal slides of your own into the sequence. Used along with this book, that slide presentation can be a catalyst in helping you explore challenging situations in your company, move teams through the higher levels of thinking, and create and innovate for results. We use the slides shown to set the stage for change workshops, frame creative-thinking sessions, and drive problem solving. Should you be interested, you can find information and a coupon on the last page in the book on how to order sets of slides from the School of Innovators.

WARNING! These slides are not intended to be illustrations for the book; they are meant to be used as a "flip-through slide show"—an overview of the 7 Levels of Change —and are in a set sequence. As you read the book you'll quickly discover that there is no direct correlation between the slides and the text on the page on which they happen to be.

THE 7 LEVELS OF CHANGE

A Strategy for Creativity, Innovation, and Continuous Improvement

Level 1: Effectiveness—
       Doing the right things

Level 2: Efficiency—
       Doing things right

Level 3: Improving—
       Doing the right things better

Level 4: Cutting—
       Doing away with things

Level 5: Copying—
       Doing things other people are doing

Level 6: Different—
       Doing things no one else is doing

Level 7: Impossible—
       Doing things that can't be done

2

GETTING RESULTS

Everyone wants to get results, and innovation is a new and different result. To be innovative you have to do things different. How do you do things different? Follow the Mindshift Model below, reading first from left to right. How do you get differ-

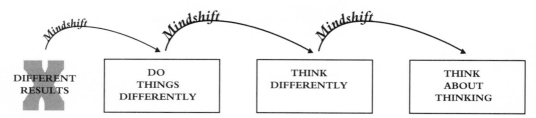

ent results? From doing things different. That requires a mindshift. How do you do things different? You have to think different. There's a second-order mindshift. How do you think different? You have to think about thinking. That's a third-order mindshift. Thinking about thinking is the biggest mindshift of the three because the vast majority of people have never thought about the way they think.

Focus on different. What's different around you? What's different as a result of what just happened? What's different as a result of what you just did? What's different about what you just noticed? How do you notice different? Start by noticing *same*. Mornings are often mired in sameness. Notice how you wake up. Notice what you do when you wake up. Notice when you wake up. Is it the same time every day? Now, shake things up. Change something in your life that is the same every day. Do one thing different each day and notice it! Move one thing in your home or office to gradually change your perspective on what you're noticing. If you do that, you're on your way to innovation. Pick up the pace and do two things different each day and notice it. Move two things in your home. Three, four . . .

There are two main sides to the 7 Levels of Change: at work and at home. They apply everywhere we find change, everywhere in life that we have to deal with change.

LEVEL 1
Effective

Doing the Right Things

3

THE 7 LEVELS OF CHANGE AT WORK

Level 1: Effectiveness—Doing the right things
- Set priorities
- Focus!
- Do what's important first
- Become more effective

Level 2: Efficiency—Doing the right things right
- Follow procedures
- Understand standards
- Clean up your mess
- Become more efficient

Level 3: Improving—Doing things better
- Think about what you're doing
- Find ways to improve things
- Listen to suggestions
- Help, coach, and mentor others

Level 4: Cutting—Doing away with things
- Stop doing what doesn't count
- Simplify
- Ask "Why?"
- Refocus continuously

Level 5: Adapting—Doing things other people are doing
- Notice and observe more
- Read about best practices
- Think before you think
- Copy!

Level 6: Diffferent—Doing things no one else is doing
- Think about thinking
- Ask "Why not?"
- Combine new technologies
- Focus on different, not similar

Level 7: Impossible—Doing things that can't be done
- Question assumptions
- Defocus: Get a little crazy
- Break the rules!
- What's impossible today, but . . . ?
- Wouldn't it be amazing if . . . ?
- Where will it take real magic?

NOTE: A copy of this is on the last page in the book — cut it out and carry it with you

4

THE 7 LEVELS OF CHANGE AT HOME
Level 1: Effectiveness—Doing the right things
- Talk and communicate
- Make lists—do your chores
- Keep your promises
- Start a savings program

Level 2: Efficiency—Doing the right things right
- Start an investment plan
- Set priorities for fun
- Praise and compliment
- Actually listen

Level 3: Improving—Doing things better
- Be more loving and supportive
- Become more cost-conscious
- Develop new habits—grow
- Increase amount of savings

Level 4: Cutting—Doing away with things
- Stop impulse buying
- Stop negative "self-talk"
- Eliminate criticizing and blaming
- Simplify your life
- Detoxify your life
- Turn off the lights

Level 5: Copying—Doing things other people are doing
- Copy what works for other families
- Stick ideas on the refrigerator
- Take a real vacation
- Read, study, discuss

Level 6: Different—Doing things no one else is doing
- Try something you've never tried
- Get professional help
- Mentally incorporate your family: We, Inc.
- Go on a family adventure

Level 7: Impossible—Doing things that can't be done
- Dream the impossible dream
- Wouldn't it be great if we . . . ?
- Enjoy each other
- Make a dream come true

5

7 LEVELS OF THINKING

Each of the 7 Levels of Change has a corresponding mindshift, a change in thinking, that accompanies it. To do different, to make a change, you must first think different.

Level 1: Effective thinking
• Thinking that produces the intended result
• Thinking that is focused
• Thinking that exhibits a high ratio of output to input, i.e., ideas to thinking

Level 2: Efficient thinking
• Thinking that produces ideas with a minimum of waste, expense, unnecessary effort, or time
• Thinking with a specific intended or expected effect in mind
• J.I.T. Thinking

Level 3: Better thinking, positive thinking
• Thinking that is higher in quality
• Thinking that is more useful, suitable, or desirable
• Thinking that moves you forward and helps you make progress
• Thinking that is free from criticism or negativity

Level 4: Refocused thinking
• Thinking that returns you to a central concept or idea
• Thinking that helps you concentrate once more with greater intensity
• 80:20 Thinking

Level 5: Visual thinking
• Thinking that perceives with the eye, that notices
• Thinking that holds a visual image in the mind

• Thinking that believes possible, that sees, that imagines

Level 6: Lateral thinking
• Thinking that departs from the norm
• Thinking that is different in style, type, form, process, quality, amount, or nature from any other thinking
• Thinking that deliberately cuts across accepted channels of thought or patterns instead of moving up or down within them
• Thinking that reverses basic assumptions and accepted logic or reasoning
• Thinking that switches patterns within a system
• Thinking that approaches a problem from a different perspective, including backward
• Thinking that is diffferent

Level 7: Imaginative thinking
• Thinking that forms mental images that are neither perceived as real nor present to the senses
• Thinking that deals with reality by using the creative power of the mind
• Thinking that is resourceful
• Thinking that overcomes obstacles and restrictions
• Thinking that leads to innovation
• Breakout thinking
• Out-of-the-box thinking

6

THINKING ABOUT THINKING

Innovation and creativity start with ideas. We have to think before we can have an idea. To be creative, start by thinking about thinking. To be innovative, do something with your ideas.

Empty your head, clean your mind.

- First, take time out to think. If you have to, actually put it on your calendar. Block out the time, hold your calls, unplug the phone. Or find a time outside of work conducive to thinking. Go outside. Don't just do something, sit there and think. Turn off your car phone. Take a quiet hour in the morning before the rest of the family is up. Give up worrying and start thinking about thinking. Don't think about anything in particular, just open your mind to your thoughts.
- Next, become aware of how you think. Take a look again at the 7 Levels of Thinking with this in mind. Remember, innovation involves doing things different, and to do something different, you must first think different. Before you can think different, you must think about the way you think—examine your basic thinking processes. Look at the thoughts that come into your mind as you think and reflect on them—deliberately and nonjudgmentally.
- Thinking comes before doing, and thinking about thinking comes before thinking. This triple mindshift is critical if you are going to get different results.

Think about it...

Think about it...

THINKING ABOUT THINKING

Level 1 Change

Focused Thinking

fo·cus·ed (fΩ"kŌs"d) n., pl. 1. to caus
to converge on or toward a centr
point; concentrate.

ME, INC.®

Many people never take the time to think about who they are, who they have been, and who they want to become. Me, Inc.® is the deeply reflective, deliberate exercise of mentally incorporating yourself, leading you to think about yourself as a personal business venture. By mentally incorporating, you move through a structured process to create a business plan for your life.

Me, Inc.® is a change process that moves you gradually through increasing levels of personal reflection at each of the 7 Levels of Change. The process of mentally incorporating helps you take inventory of your skills, abilities, traits, and unusual qualities. It helps you define your goals, wishes, and dreams, and focuses you on your basic beliefs, values, and operating principles. It examines your experiences and your personal style to help you define a personal vision and mission. Finally, Me, Inc.® helps you get to where you want to be.

The actual exercise of mentally incorporating is not a short or quick process. It's one that requires much introspection and is described in detail at each level of change throughout the book. And it's a process that works best when done in the order I've laid it out in the 7 Levels. It's addressed as a whole in Appendix I—Me, Inc.®

Change

**What is one thing you
Really want to change?**

...BLUE SLIP

INNOVATE OR DIE!

Today our thinking *must* shift. The world we live in is changing so rapidly that to survive, we must continually change how we see it and how we think about it. Consider change and the rate of change in your own lifetime. Remember your home when you were growing up—when households had only one telephone? When there was no dial on the telephone and you had to call the operator? Only one television? Only a few channels on the television set? Only one bathroom? Only one car? No computer?

Today we're constantly in touch with information beamed by satellites around the world and sent through the Internet and over digital wireless communication. Clinton's run for the White House, the Republican takeover of Congress, even advertising campaigns for consumer goods all are riding the waves of the desire for change, ever creating a new shoreline that is this country.

And if we think the rate of change has escalated rapidly over the past two or three decades, get ready to shift into high gear—the ride has only just begun.

For businesses large and small, being proactive with change—being innovative and striving for continuous improvement—is key to survival and growth in the new millennium. It's "Innovate or Die!" None of us wants to become a monolith, however, so many of today's corporations and organizations—built on yesterday's ideas—are continuing to live on those ideas today. Unless we innovate and continually change, we'll turn to stone and become memorials to our past. We'll die. It's that simple.

I consciously began focusing on innovation in 1984, while I was a colonel in the U.S. Air Force and director of long-range planning for Electronic Security Command (now called the Air Force Intelligence Agency). Driven by change in technology and change in the world, the air force launched an initiative deliberately focused on innovation. As the long-range planner, I was asked to develop a corporate

> *"The world we created today has problems which cannot be solved by thinking the way we thought when we created them."*
>
> **Albert Einstein**

10

strategy paper and action plan to implement the initiative and translate innovation into a corporate value. I started by creating an Innovation Center to serve as a catalyst for ideas and as an extension of our long-range planning staff.

Within six months, the Innovation Center and I were spun off from long-range planning, and I became director of the Office of Innovation, with the mission of sparking innovation throughout the command. We rapidly developed a worldwide network of innovation centers focused on operational innovation in the field. By the time I retired, I was known as Colonel Innovation; even my air force name tag said "Innovation" rather than "Smith."

Surprisingly to me, this run at "Innovate or Die!" was a natural transition to civilian life and into some of the world's largest corporations. From 1987 through 1991, I was a contract executive with Exxon Corporation, with a mandate to stimulate creativity and innovative thinking throughout the organization—no different from my charter in the air force. Starting in Exxon Marketing where we created an Innovation Center along the lines of the air force model, the drive for innovation spread into virtually every area of the company.

In 1988, I created the School for Innovators to develop and train change agents and innovators in Exxon. Two years later it became an "open" school, drawing innovators primarily from Fortune 100 companies and working on real-world issues and problems facing them. Today we have graduates not only at Exxon but also at IBM, DuPont, AT&T, Proctor & Gamble, General Mills, Chase Manhattan Bank, Steelcase, R. J. Reynolds, Karastan Carpet, KFC, public schools, the U.S. Air Force, and the U.S. Navy.

One of the most important ideas to come out of the School for Innovators is the 7 Levels of Change. The 7 Levels evolved over several years as I was thinking about how to connect creativity, innovation, and continuous improvement. Each of these goals—common to my clients in corporate America and all of us as individuals striving to succeed in life—shares common themes. It struck me that they are all

The School for Innovators — R&D for the 7 levels of change process

Change

What is one thing you Really want to change?

...BLUE SLIP

about ideas. Creativity is about having ideas, and innovation and continuous improvement are about implementing ideas.

Ideas are about change. When you implement a new idea, you cause a change. This led me to insights about the different sizes and levels of change. Adapting the work of quality gurus W. Edwards Deming and William Conway and working with some of the country's greatest management minds—our clients—the 7 Levels gradually evolved from three initial levels to five levels to seven and its present form. The number "7" was not a deliberate choice but one arrived at over time. It works.

Change can be very difficult for companies of any size as well as for individuals. By breaking down change into different levels for my clients, I found them phenomenally successful at making significant changes that affected not only the company's bottom line but also its future path of success. In the School for Innovators, I found our graduates making profound changes in their lives. When we integrated the structure of the 7 Levels of Change into Me, Inc.® (the process we developed to help our graduates set new strategic directions and mentally incorporate themselves), they exploded with energy, commitment, and self-confidence.

Continuously searching for ways to reduce fear of change in order to move groups and individuals more quickly through higher levels of perceived risk, we entered into a strategic relationship with Mike Donahue, director of the Colorado Mountain School in Estes Park. In 1991 we integrated rock climbing into a School for Innovators for IBM and achieved some amazing mindshifts. We had discovered how to move people to Level 6, *different*, and Level 7, *impossible*, first on the personal level and then on the business level, with amazing effect.

In 1994, sparked by the insights we were gaining by using the 7 Levels of Change coupled with rock climbing and low-level mountaineering in the School for Innovators, I hit on the idea of "Thinking Expeditions" to operationalize the 7 Levels and leverage the ongoing stream of discoveries, learnings, tools, and techniques coming out of the school. We began to

11

Ideas = Change...

12

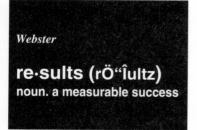

Thinking Expeditions move corporate Teams through the 7 Levels of change

design Thinking Expeditions built around a wide variety of real world challenges facing some of the world's largest corporations—Exxon, ARCO, British Petroleum, Proctor and Gamble, WMX Technologies, Hoechst Celanese Corporation, General Mills, and the U.S. Navy's SMART SHIP—and led teams to achieve startling and exciting breakthrough results over the whole range of the 7 Levels of Change.

With every Thinking Expedition, we have developed new techniques, new tools, and new approaches for each level of change, both out of sheer necessity and also by building on the learnings of previous expedition. Those discoveries and learnings are what this book is about. This book explains those tools and techniques in detail, in the context of how to use them, and when to use them at different levels of change. When you're finished with the book, you'll have your own tool kit for change loaded and ready to go on expedition.

By gaining insight into the 7 Levels of Change and by learning the tools to use at each level, I believe extraordinary summits, exciting discoveries, and results can be yours.

Climb on!

Webster

re·sults (rŏ"îultz)
noun. a measurable success

THE 7 LEVELS OF CHANGE

LEVEL 1: Doing the right things
LEVEL 2: Doing things right
LEVEL 3: Doing things better
LEVEL 4: Stopping doing things
LEVEL 5: Doing things other people are doing
LEVEL 6: Doing things no one else is doing
LEVEL 7: Doing things that can't be done

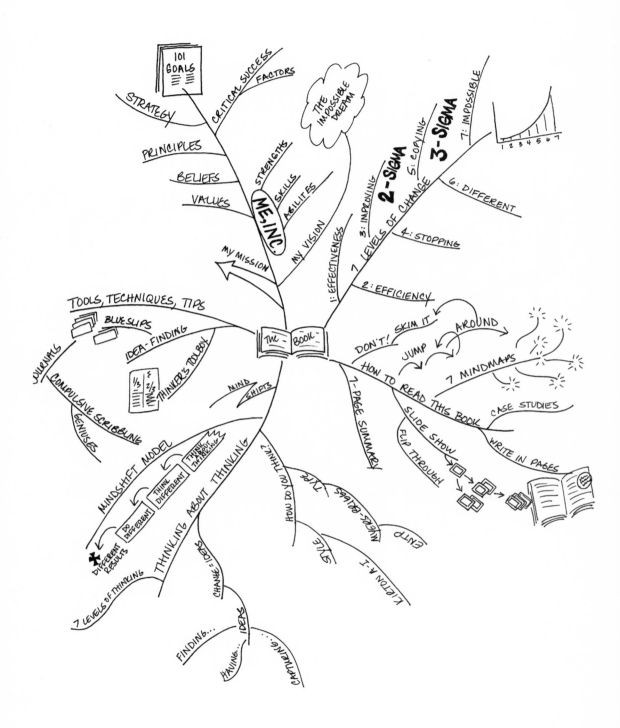

THE MAGIC NUMBER 7

The 7 Levels of Change actually started out as three levels and evolved to 7. After many changes, additions, and subtractions, I arrived at the present version, which has remained stable for some time, primarily because it works.

In my work with large corporations, I have found several other lists that help my clients think out of the box. Guess what? They're each lists of seven elements:

7 DIFFERENTIATORS IN UNUSUAL THINKERS
Rolf Smith
1. Noticing: An awareness of diffferent
2. Openness: The ability to suspend judgment, clear the mind
3. Playfulness: The ability to play with ideas
4. Connecting: The ability to make idea-connections
5. Tension: Continuous divergence-convergence
6. Quantity: Many different kinds of ideas
7. Compression: The ability to headline concepts

THE 7 PRINCIPLES OF BREAKTHROUGH THINKING
Gerald Nadler & Shozo Hibino
1. Every problem is unique
2. Focus on purpose
3. Solution-after-next thinking
4. System-of-problems perspective
5. Limit information collection
6. People involvement in the design
7. Betterment timeline: Continual change

After living with the 7 Levels of Change for a couple of years, I'm convinced that there is something mystical about the number "7." Among gamblers, it's a favorite lucky number—among authors, too, it seems.

And apparently it has some scientific basis. Knowing I had been a math major in college, a friend of mine, at E-Systems in Dallas, Chuck Brodnax, once sent me an old paper entitled, "The Magic Number 7 plus or minus 2." It was written around 1949, as I recall, and was based on research that showed people max out at remembering seven digits or things. After that, retention drops off quickly. Oddly enough (maybe not?) it's also used as a

16

rule of thumb in brainstorming and creative problem solving, where we tell people to limit their ideas or problem statements to seven words. And it seems to have been applied to the thinking behind telephone numbers. Following are some more useful lists of "7."

THE 7 CULTURAL FORCES THAT DEFINE AMERICANS
Josh Hammond & James Morrison
1. Insistence on choice
2. Pursuit of impossible dreams
3. Obsession with BIG and MORE
4. Impatience with time
5. Acceptance of mistakes
6. The urge to improvise
7. Fixation on what's new

THE 7 HUMAN INTELLIGENCES
Howard Gardner
1. Linguistic
2. Logical–Mathematical
3. Spatial
4. Musical
5. Bodily Kinesthetic
6. Interpersonal (Others)
7. Intrapersonal (Self)

THE 7 HABITS OF HIGHLY SUCCESSFUL PEOPLE
Stephen Covey
1. Be Proactive
2. Begin with the End in Mind
3. Put First Things First
4. Think Win/Win
5. Seek First to Understand
6. Synergize: Creative Cooperation
7. Sharpen the Saw

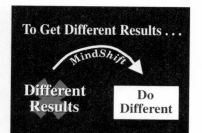

THE 7 MAJOR CHANGES
Shad Helmstetter
1. Loss
2. Separation
3. Relocation
4. A Change in Relationship
5. A Change in Direction
6. A Change in Health
7. Personal Growth

THE 7 HUMAN NEEDS
Abraham Maslow
1. Physiological
2. Security and Safety
3. Love and Feelings of Belonging
4. Competence, Prestige, and Esteem
5. Autonomy and Independence
6. Self-Actualization and Fulfillment
7. Curiosity and Understanding

17

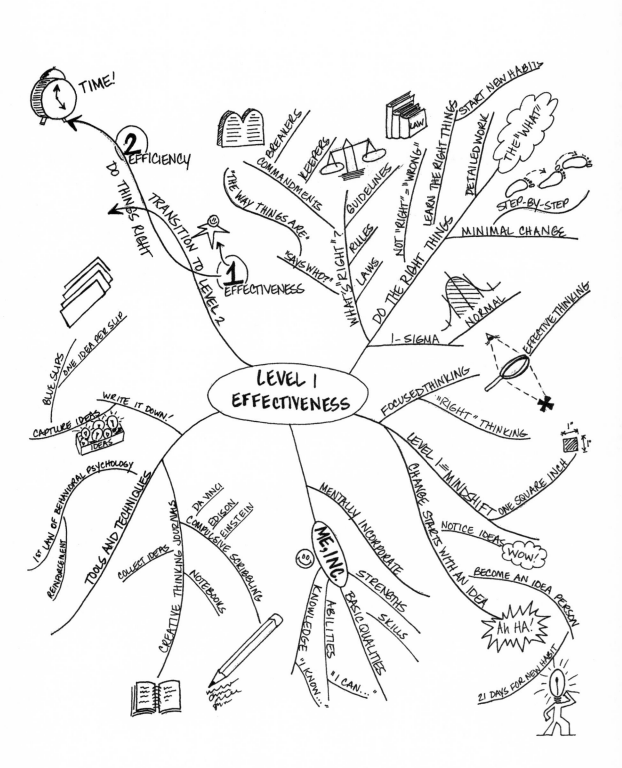

LEVEL 1: EFFECTIVENESS

UNDERSTANDING LEVEL 1

Imagine yourself on the first day of a new job. Typically, whether you are an executive or a worker on the line, you are highly focused on learning the basics of the job—the "what" that makes up the job. This is fundamental Level 1 change—doing the right things and being effective. Those first few days are full of Level 1 doing—familiarizing yourself with the mission of your group, who's who and who you work with, what they do, the technology in the office, the phones and other communications systems, the location of the watercooler and the rest rooms. The right things. The what.

LEVEL 1 CHANGES ARE ABOUT STARTING NEW HABITS

In most cases, your new boss or a supervisor or an old hand who understands everything walks you around and helps you understand what the right things are, how things work, rules, roles, and focus. There are a lot of new ideas for you, and you either pay very close attention or you write them down because you've got to turn them into changes in you—new habits. Of course

you didn't fall off a turnip truck when you took the new job. You know a lot of things, too, and have some pretty solid experience behind you. And you can draw on that. It turns out that the basics—the right things—are pretty much the right things everywhere. So these early changes you have to go through in a new job are predominantly incremental, relatively small, and involve low risk and low effort to get up to speed. Still, they are changes.

Where does change come from? Change starts with an idea. When you're learning all the right things in a new job, they're coming to you as ideas at the thinking level. When you begin doing them, you transition the ideas into personal changes. Ideas are a basic part of change. So in a sense, part of doing the right thing on a new job is becoming an idea person and paying attention to a lot of new ideas.

If you are going to become aware of change, you have to become aware of ideas. If becoming an idea person is doing the right thing, then collecting ideas, getting ideas, is a Level 1 change. Ideas are everywhere; you only have to capture them.

20

R – Take one Blue Slip before each meal for the next 21 days...

LEVEL 1 TOOL #1: WRITE IT DOWN!

Writing down ideas is doing the right thing. For a lot of people who don't already make a habit of recording their ideas, that's a Level 1 change. Ideas are in magazines, books, and newspapers. The first step: Tear out ideas and collect them. The next step: Remember to write down ideas when you have them. Win Wenger, in his book *The Einstein Factor*, highlights the first law of behavioral psychology: Whatever you reinforce you will get more of. Every time you write down an idea you reinforce the importance of having ideas, of being an idea person. And, whenever you don't write down an idea, you reinforce the behavior of not being an idea person. This is again about habits. It takes twenty-one days to establish a new habit or to replace an old habit with a new one—a change.

LEVEL 1 TOOL #2: BLUE SLIPS

The most basic tool at Level 1 is a simple piece of paper that I call a Blue Slip. It's just a small blue piece of paper, unlined, that can fit into your shirt pocket—smaller than a 3x5 card. I use them to collect ideas. (Many similar tools can help you. A notebook, a special place in your Day-Timer just for ideas, a tape recorder, your computer, Post-it Notes.) Where did the idea for Blue Slips come from? We developed them as part of our long-range planning process in the air force.

Where do Blue Slips come from? They're not at your local office supply warehouse, at least not as Blue Slips. But they're easy to produce there. Just get a ream of light blue 8 ½-inch by 11-inch paper and cut it in half horizontally. Cut the halves into quarters, producing eight Blue Slips per sheet of paper. Any corner print shop can do this for you, getting you four thousand Blue Slips per ream—enough for quite a few ideas! While we don't completely understand why, the size (not the typical 3x5 card size, but 2¾ x 4¼ instead) *is* important. You tend not to fill it up—you keep the ideas brief and focused. The fact that Blue Slips are unlined has also been a real creativity booster—you're not forced to a particular size of writing. They are just large enough to develop short bursts of ideas, yet too small for writing complete sentences or long paragraphs. They also fit nicely into shirt pockets, better than 3x5 cards.

Webster

in·no·va·tion (^{9}n"Ö-v$\geq$"shÖn)
noun. a new and different result

Why are Blue Slips blue? Empirically, they seem to consistently lead to more ideas than writing on white paper or any other colored paper. When they are strewn across a desk with other papers, they show up well. Finally, they are distinctive enough that any time you see them they remind you of ideas and thinking.

The power of Blue Slips lies in capturing each idea on a separate slip that you can play with, shuffle around with other ideas, make connections to, or pull out of your pocket and show someone. You can't do that as freely with a notebook.

Put ideas on your mental agenda. Become a compulsive scribbler. Many highly creative people, inventors, and geniuses in history were known for being compulsive scribblers. Turn your scribbles into a journal. Journaling is a great way to give your creativity a jump-start. Blue Slips and Creative Thinking Journals are among the first pieces of gear we issue people on a Thinking Expedition or in our School for Innovators. Michael Roberts, operations manager for Kentucky Fried Chicken in England and Northern Ireland and a graduate of the School for Innovators, says that journaling helps him "keep on keeping on."

"By recording ideas and insights, the rate of questions, ideas, and change accelerates. The difference in two days' journals demonstrates your improving creativity. At first your approach is slow. After time, you begin to make the ascent," Roberts says.

Ray Holbrook, Commissioners Court judge for Galveston County, Texas, and another School for Innovators alumnus, says Blue Slips are a breakthrough on the way to becoming an innovator. "They provide a means for preserving ideas and thoughts and also drum up those things. Journaling is more deliberate and thoughtful," he says. "It's used to develop ideas and thoughts and gives you a permanent record of progress on a project. Both practices can be invaluable if you are looking to grow personally and professionally."

Leonardo da Vinci, Thomas Edison, Albert Einstein, Michael Faraday were compulsive scribblers, and all kept extensive journals or notebooks of some sort.

21

Tip! Play with your ideas

Develop the habit of scribbling down ideas and thoughts

22

Buy a journal — start scribbling now!

LEVEL 1 TOOL #3: CREATIVE THINKING JOURNALS

A journal is not a diary. It's a tool for regularly recording ideas, thoughts, and observations on your thinking processes. A journal is about insights, introspection, and reflection—not analysis and data collection. Journals are for deep thoughts, and, in fact, I call ours "A Tool for Personal Learning and Growth." And yet, they're a simple tool, nothing more than a small book of blank pages. There's no right or wrong way to keep a Creative Thinking Journal beyond just doing it as the right thing to do—a Level 1 change.

In November 1995, we designed and ran a Thinking Expedition School for Innovators for Johnson & Johnson's entire Executive Development Group. Gerry Kells, director of the group, focused the expedition on exploring "the core of the core"—the critical core values that make Johnson & Johnson what it is as a company—and how to teach that in a whole new program that would become Johnson & Johnson's worldwide executive development program. The J&J team connected very strongly with the Creative Thinking Journal process and introspection around personal values and beliefs. Since the School for Innovators, Johnson & Johnson has implemented its first version of the new Executive Development Program called "Framework for Growth"—and incorporated Creative Thinking Journals into it. We view the use of Thinking Journals as a simple Level 1 change, and Johnson & Johnson's adapting journals for their Executive Development classes as basic Level 5 copying and adapting. Yet, for Johnson & Johnson, it was clear Level 6 change—something no one had ever done before and very, very different for them culturally. Keeping a journal is not the same level of change for some people that it is for others. Perspective, creative style, psychological type, and culture all bring perspective and relativity to change.

Generally speaking, Level 1 is about maintaining the status quo in a positive sense. In major manufacturing companies that produce products on a line, maintaining the status quo means producing that widget over and over and over. The company is not about creating new stuff; it is about producing this one

> "The significant problems we face cannot be solved at the same level we were at when we created them"
>
> *Albert Einstein*

thing as effectively and efficiently as possible. A major piece of what goes on in any manufacturing company is doing and thinking at Level 1 and Level 2, being effective and efficient.

It's in fact vital to have Level 1 and 2 thinkers doing very structured tasks on a production line. Detailed work is their passion. A Level 1 doer will complete his task to perfection but might not say anything about the broken part that came his way. That's not his job. The Level 2 doer, however, will stop the line and raise the question, which may or may not be the most efficient way to run the line.

The trouble is that after changing, some people then stay at Level 1 thinking and doing. They don't move to Level 2—it's too big a change for them. It's easy to recognize people who operate primarily at Level 1. They're detail oriented and task oriented, structured, targeted, and conscientious. They're focused on their interpretation of what the right things are. They're strong rule followers and black-and-white thinkers who like to gather the facts. They respond best to specific instructions. They know their job description and will perform to the letter of it. But don't ask them to stretch outside of that job description box—they typically are not prone to that degree of innovation (which is how they see it). As a result, they may sometimes appear to be close-minded and probably won't have a wealth of original ideas.

Most Level 1 changes are small, incremental changes. As you move up to Level 7, the changes typically become more fundamental changes that affect the whole system as opposed to the details of the system. Borrowing from physics, the lower level changes can be described as first-order changes—a change of position, moving from point A to point B. As you move toward Level 7, the changes become second-order changes, a change in speed, constantly accelerating as you go from point A to point B.

A while back I took a picture of three pay telephones at a gas station. A change in them really caught my eye. Two are regular height, and one is low for wheelchair or child use—a great example of doing the right thing, Level 1

Big ah HA!
— not all changes
are the same

24

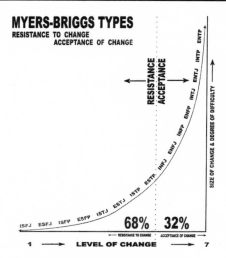

MYERS-BRIGGS TYPES
RESISTANCE TO CHANGE
ACCEPTANCE OF CHANGE

RESISTANCE ← | → ACCEPTANCE

SIZE OF CHANGE & DEGREE OF DIFFICULTY →

ENTP
INTP
ENTJ
INTJ
ENFP
ENFJ
INFP
INFJ
ESTP
ISTP
ESTJ
ISTJ
ESFP
ISFP
ESFJ
ISFJ

68% | **32%**

← RESISTANCE TO CHANGE | ACCEPTANCE OF CHANGE →

1 → **LEVEL OF CHANGE** → 7

Effectiveness. It's not more efficient or a clear improvement, but it's effective and the right thing to do to accommodate more people and enlarge the customer base.

Level 1 changes can be more fundamental, too, if you are redefining what is right. AT&T, the great-grandmother of the pay telephone, for instance, has been in the long distance business for decades, but if the company is going to make a change and get into the global information business, then it has to redefine what is right. The entire focus of the company must change from long distance itself to information moving over long distance—a fundamental, Level 1 change that has the potential, relatively, to also be a Level 6 *Different* change or Level 7 Impossible change.

ROLF'S THEORY OF RELATIVITY

All changes are relative. What is right for you isn't always right for me. It could be a much bigger kind of right thing to you than it is to me. Different people see the right things differently. What's the correct way to put on a roll of toilet paper—with the loose end coming over the top of the roll or from underneath the roll? You'd be surprised how strongly people view this. Want to experiment? Next time you're

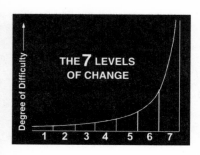

THE **7** LEVELS
OF CHANGE

Degree of Difficulty →

1 2 3 4 5 6 7

at someone else's house, turn the toilet paper roll around, wait until after your hostess goes to the bathroom, and bring up the topic. "I noticed the toilet paper was on backwards so I reversed it for you…"

If you are naturally a structured person who is a rule follower, check your rule-following index with speeding. Doing the right thing is obeying speed limits. In fact, it's the law, which means it's really right! But, how much over the speed limit do you drive? If you are at the other end of the scale, very unstructured, breaking the rules may be doing the right thing. You may consider speed limits guidelines or even unneccessary (like they do in Montana), while the more structured person would be horrified and considers breaking the speed limits a Level 7 change—the impossible.

So, just how much over the speed limit do you drive?

THINKING ABOUT THINKING

Think about it: to get right results you have to do right. To do right you have to think right. Think about your thinking at this level. It's about focus. What is the right thing to focus on? Typically, it's one thing at a time. Right thinking is fitting, proper, and appropriate. It's thinking that produces the intended result. It's thinking that's in accordance with fact, reason, truth, or the commonly accepted way. Effective thinking is thinking that gets an intended or expected effect, thinking that produces the intended result. It's 1-Sigma thinking, meaning that on the normal curve, it's inside the "normal" range. Take a look at the diagram below. About 68 percent of the time, you will be thinking in the "normal" or 1-Sigma range: Level 1 Effectiveness, Level 2 Efficiency, and Level 3 Improving in terms of change.

When you move past Level 3, you move over into 2-Sigma or "interesting" thinking, where you'll find 28 percent of change sits: Level 4 Cutting and Level 5 Copying. This is a shift from incremental change into fundamental change.

Finally, the smallest percentage of thinking, about 5 percent, lies at 3-Sigma and beyond, out at the ends of the

Have you ever thought about the way you think?

26

The Normal Distribution

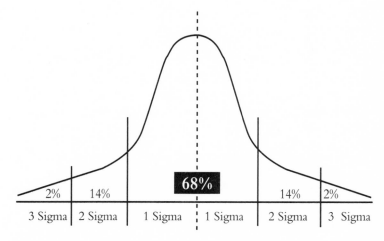

2%	14%		68%		14%	2%
3 Sigma	2 Sigma	1 Sigma		1 Sigma	2 Sigma	3 Sigma

normal curve. That's where Level 6 and Level 7 change comes from, the different and impossible, with corresponding quantum changes in performance.

When you are thinking about your thinking at Level 1, you constantly have to back up and ask yourself, "Is my thinking focused on doing something that will produce the right thing?" "Are we getting the expected effect?" You look at the result and the effect. It means you have to have some clear definitions about what is right. Ask yourself what you have defined as "right" for you and for the job you are working on.

Rock climbing is a good example of right or effective thinking. In rock climbing, to be safe you have to focus on doing the right thing. You have to focus on your partner while your partner is climbing, anticipating what he or she is going to do—what move he's going to make. You focus on one thing at a time, so you're thinking about the most important, most right thing to do at any one point in time. You focus only on where you're going to put your foot or your toe or where your next move is going to be. You focus on the one square inch that is *now*.

THE 7 LEVELS OF CHANGE

LEVEL 1: Doing the right things
LEVEL 2: Doing things right
LEVEL 3: Doing things better
LEVEL 4: Stopping doing things
LEVEL 5: Doing things other people are doing
LEVEL 6: Doing things no one else is doing
LEVEL 7: Doing things that can't be done

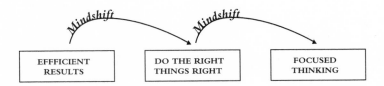

MINDSHIFT
Level 1:

The above diagram illustrates Level 1 thinking and the mindshifts you must make to achieve results at Level 1. If you are going to do the right things, you have to make a mindshift and focus on what they are and not allow yourself to be distracted.

To make a Level 1 change, if you are thinking about your thinking, you will notice a new definition of what is right, commit it to memory, and move from thinking to doing with a new perspective on what is right.

PROS & CONS

Every level of change has pros and cons. The positive aspects of Level 1 are easy to see. When you are thinking and doing and changing at Level 1, you are very focused, and results are often immediate. You learn the right things to do at your new job and then you do them, often learning from a co-worker or mentor. The right results happen. The negative of staying at this level is that you generally aren't bringing much thinking into it at this point. You are just doing what you have been told to do. You become so focused on learning these right things that you don't pay much attention to anything else. Level 1 thinking can act as a negative filter for other things, bigger changes.

When you are doing the right things, you are helping the existing processes along because this is a proven way that

28

Me, Inc.
who am I?

works. Carried to the extreme—being totally focused on what's "right"—can become a negative if it closes you off to new ideas and other "right" things.

ME, INC.®

At each level of change, I'm going to give you a Me, Inc.® exercise to get you moving on the way to mentally incorporating yourself. The process of mentally incorporating is an introspective exercise that helps you develop a personal mission statement, take inventory of your values and strengths, determine your Critical Success Factors, come up with 101 personal goals, and create a vision of the future for you.

Me, Inc.® is an entrepreneurial business built on your personal values, strengths, experiences, and ideas. As you mentally incorporate, you will discover your own power to focus your mission and strategy and learn how to continuously improve. You will explore how you are unique and different and question assumptions you make about yourself. For more on Me, Inc.® see Appendix I.

To begin the process of Me, Inc.® at Level 1, reflect on yourself and the basic qualities that you have. Think about your strengths and skills and abilities, things you do well, things you know, things that make you what you are. Make a list of them—at least one full page. With this list in front of you, try to define your purpose in life—what your focus is. Make a rough cut at your purpose and plan to come back later and refine it.

TRANSITION TO LEVEL 2: FROM WHAT TO HOW

As you master the right things and feel comfortable with what your role and your new job are, you'll begin to change. You'll find that you begin to think about how to do the right things right. Here you begin to transition into a Level 2 change—efficiency. Now you begin to think about how to do the particular aspects of your job, about how to save time, about how not to waste energy or money, about speed, method, and process.

When doing the right things becomes second nature—

On Expedition!

BIG Change

Do you realize...
...how much time it takes to adjust to BIG changes?

reflexive—it's easy to move into Level 2 changes and learn how to do the right things right. With the right things mastered, you can begin to start noticing relationships, procedures, and processes. Your boss or mentors will point out more efficient ways to accomplish things. You'll come up with efficiencies as well, and you'll intuitively know it's time to move to Level 2.

29

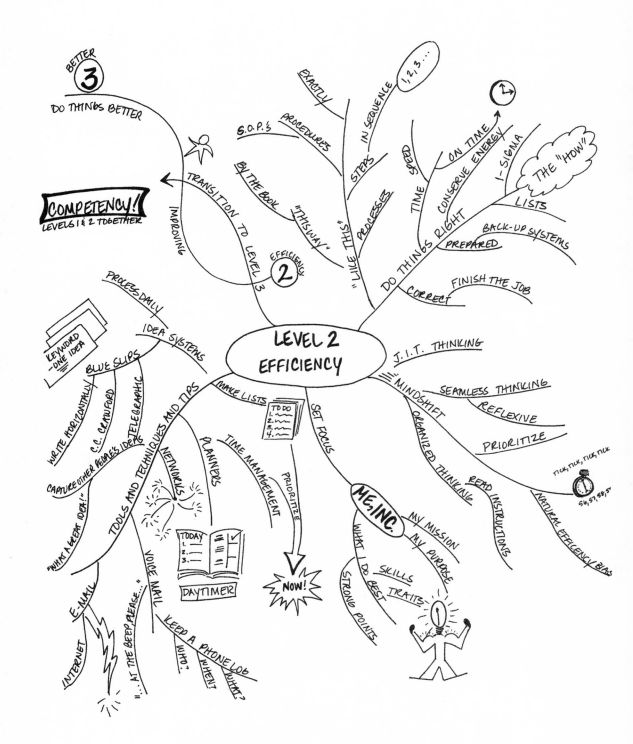

LEVEL 2: EFFICIENCY

UNDERSTANDING LEVEL 2

You've mastered the status quo, "the way things are around here." You're doing the right things, the "what" of your new job. Now it's time for change—doing the right things right. You begin to focus on "how" to do your job—the efficiencies, saving time and effort, money, and resources. This is Level 2 thinking, and the changes that result from this type of thinking can make a phenomenal difference in the everyday life of a company.

People operating at Level 2 are easily recognizable. They read instructions and regulations, trying to get at exactly the right way to complete tasks. They ask for tips on how to do things best. They're not big picture thinkers when they're in Level 2 mode; instead, they're thinking sequentially, looking for a glitch in efficiency. If you give them a list of things to do, they'll ask you which one to do first, then prioritize the list, and complete the tasks in that order.

Buttoned-up and on time, they'll have a clean desk with sharpened pencils lined up and ready to go. In the center of the desk will be their task at hand. When they're finished, it goes in the file, and they're on to the next task. Unless it's lunchtime. Lunch is probably at the same time every day. So is quitting time. Time is a big driver for Level 2 thinking.

If you give them a proposal to look at and ask for comments, before you get feedback on content, they'll tell you there's a misspelling on page six and give you all of the punctuation errors. If they're not on time for meetings, they're five minutes early and are religious about using their time manager or calendar. If they've agreed to a thirty-minute meeting with you, at twenty-nine minutes, watch out! They're already putting away their file folder because they won't need it for your closing comment (not comments!).

Level 2 doers are great at finding ways to conserve time and energy and resources. They'll combine errands and tasks that can be completed in a logical sequence and won't stop until they find the most efficient way to do something. Then they'll make up rules surrounding what they have deemed as "doing the right things right." Such as, when the gasoline tank indicator drops below a quarter tank, it's time to fill up. Or when there are only two printer cartridges left in the drawer, it's time to stock up. You'll never find a Level 2 doer scrambling for

32

paper or supplies on deadline. They're always prepared. After all, it saves time.

Is this bad? Is it anal retentive? No—absolutely not! But it can drive people who tend to operate at higher levels of change nuts because they have great difficulty doing it. It's not their thinking style; it's not in their psychological type or makeup. Yet, time is one of the seven most important factors in the "Stuff that Americans" are made of.

LEVEL 2 TOOL #1: LISTS

Turn a Blue Slip vertically, write "To Do" and the date on the top, and make a list of the things you want to do tomorrow. Then stretch a little and add the things you *have* to do tomorrow.

LEVEL 2 TOOL #2: DAY-TIMER/PLANNER

If Blue Slip lists aren't focused and organized enough to suit you, go to your nearest office supply store and buy a loose-leaf planner, Day-Timer, time manager, or simple little notebook. If you do buy one of them, you're probably serious enough about time to read the instructions on how to "manage" it. In a nutshell, they're all the same: Write things down, use a priority system to force yourself to do the most important right things first. Write your goals in it. Over time, study your patterns. Notice what you do and don't do.

When I first started working with Exxon Corporation back in 1987, I became close friends with Peter Hearl, an Australian expatriate on a career-broadening assignment from Esso. Peter kept himself focused and on task with an impressive little loose-leaf time manager system. When Peter was made the coordinator of the Innovations Group, one of the first innovations he implemented was time management training, a clear Level 2 efficiency change. Easy and fast to put in place, it struck a chord with Exxon values. It was also personally valuable, and people had some choices. They were offered three different time management classes by three different companies, so it was easy to sell. After completing the classes, the marketing department was full of

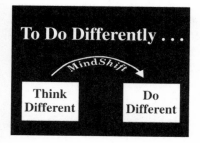

Level 2 thinking. The biggest visible change: Everyone started carrying Day-Timers. I still carry mine today, and Peter Hearl and I are still friends—despite it. And Peter is CEO of KFC/Pizza Hut in Australia/New Zealand and Southern Africa!

LEVEL 2 TOOL #3: BLUE SLIPS

(See Level 1 Tool #2 on page 22) Using Blue Slips is doing the right thing—capturing ideas. Using Blue Slips in certain ways is doing the right thing right. Blue-Slipping is a process I developed in the U.S. Air Force to facilitate long-range planning. It's an incredibly simple way to capture ideas and an efficient way to facilitate J.I.T (Just In Time) thinking and idea gathering in meetings. Blue-Slipping in groups and meetings has some immediate advantages. It's anonymous and naturally suspends judgment by the group, so it creates a fearless atmosphere that prompts out-of-the-box ideas to come forward. It helps avoid "groupthink" and yet involves all of the group's participants.

And—right things right—there are five basic rules for how to use a Blue Slip.

Tip! Blue Slips are THE Big Tool for becoming an "Idea Person"

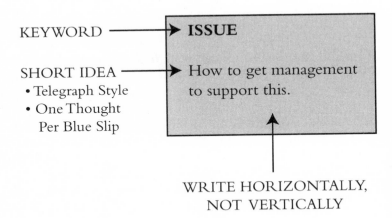

KEYWORD ⟶ **ISSUE**

SHORT IDEA ⟶ How to get management
• Telegraph Style   to support this.
• One Thought
  Per Blue Slip

WRITE HORIZONTALLY,
NOT VERTICALLY

1. You should write horizontally, not vertically, on the rectangular Blue Slip. While it can be argued that horizontal

34

is best for ideas and vertical for lists (see Level 2 Tool #1), the real reason to do this is that it makes sorting the Blue Slips easier if all of them are oriented the same way. Over time, I have discovered that people develop ideas more easily when working on a horizontal plane. I don't know why that is, it just is.

2. Write a key word in the upper left-hand corner of the Blue Slip. That focuses the idea you're putting on the slip and helps you group ideas later by key words related to a central question or problem.

3. Only one idea per Blue Slip—don't try to economize or save paper. No writing two or three ideas on a Blue Slip. This is not to limit the number of ideas you can have, but rather to keep each idea separate so you can "play" with it more easily. This will also help you sort and process the Blue Slips later.

4. Ideas and thoughts on Blue Slips should be in brief, telegraphic style, a phrase, key words, or an incomplete sentence. And no more than one. In other words, write the way you think—in short bursts of information.

5. Write legibly. It will increase the likelihood of idea connections and help you to more quickly understand and process ideas later on.

Carry Blue Slips and a pen or pencil with you at all times. Plan to have some ideas! The first thing I do every morning when I get dressed is pick up the stack of Blue Slips I had next to the bed the night before, put them in my shirt pocket, and put my pen in my pants pocket. I *know* I'm going to capture some great ideas each day. Yep, Sundays, too. Take them to church with you. You might hear a great sermon.

Focus on Change

- Think about change
- Notice change
- Become aware of change

LEVEL 2 TECHNIQUE #1: PROCESSING BLUE SLIPS

At the end of the day, I try to sit down and sort through my Blue Slips. I make a stack of ideas that can be converted quickly to actions. This is my hot, "do it NOW" list. I also make a second stack of interesting ideas that I don't know what to do with—but they're still kind of hot. Then I

35

create a third stack of ideas that are interesting, but—they're long-range ideas; I don't exactly know what to do with them right now. The first stack I convert into a list of changes to be made or things to do, then toss the Blue Slips. The long-range ideas go into a blue laundry basket in my office to be acted on later. The random ideas go back in my pocket with my blank Blue Slips. Eventually, other ideas will come along and connect with these, and they'll be converted to action or relegated to the long-range plans. This system works for me. You need to develop a personal system of your own that works for you and your ideas.

Tip!

Use Blue Slips to immediately create rapport with a customer or client. When they say something you find interesting—pull out a Blue Slip and write it down. Say, "What a great idea!" Put their name on the Blue Slip. (I always credit the people I get great ideas from.) You've just sent them a very strong message that you thought what they said was important. It's a compliment they won't forget. Want to change your life? Write down something your spouse or your significant other or one of your children says. You'll be amazed at the impact.

Another form of Level 2 change is delegating. Delegating can apply at any level, in your personal life, at home, at the office, in companies large and small. If there are too many things to do and too few people to do them, get help from others, reach outside. Delegating saves time and opens up time that can be used for thinking creatively.

I like to climb. In rock climbing, you delegate a lot of things to your belayer, your partner, so you can focus on the climb. You delegate safety and protection largely to your belayer. It's an efficient way to deal with worry and risk. But it's also built on the more basic aspects of Level 2 change— doing the right things right (which is not just about efficiency). You can't just tie knots in your climbing rope or your anchor system, you have to tie the right knots for that particular function—and you have to tie the right knots right.

[handwritten margin note:] Tip! "Develop a system for "doing something" with your ideas... —play with them

[handwritten margin note:] Wow! write down things people say when they say them —powerful compliment

36

The figure eight is the first knot most climbers learn and the most widely used. It ties them, personally, through their harness, into the end of the rope. If it's not right, you can fall a long way. The figure eight is used to clip into the middle of a rope or for connecting into anchors. You double-check the knots you tie and then your belaying partner checks them. That's doing the right things right. Pretty focused Level 2 doing.

Double-checking is doing the right things right. It takes time. It may not feel efficient. But it's the right thing to do right.

Using networks is another right thing to do right, and it can help you be extremely efficient. Within a company, develop your own network by getting a feel for who the key people are who have skills that you don't have, or who can do some special thing very well indeed. When you hit a deadline crunch, draw on your network to get things done fast. I always make it a point to get to know the graphic arts and video folks and photographers. They're always fun to work with, have a great eye for different, and can really work unusual magic for you.

LEVEL 2 TOOL #4: VOICE MAIL

This is a technology tool that gives you real time leverage. If used intelligently, it can bring incredible efficiency and time savings to you on a daily basis. Technique is an integral part of voice mail: Use voice mail deliberately, not accidentally. Accidentally is when you call people and get their voice mail. Deliberately is when you call at a time when you *know* you're going to get their voice mail. Leave details, specific questions, requests for specific information, etc., with the full intention of their calling you back to leave you a voice mail as well—with the answers you need. Get in the habit of not answering the phone in periods when you're typically productive and efficient. Unplug it! You don't have to answer it—those days are gone. If it's unplugged you won't be tempted. Let it roll into your voice mail system.

Don't answer the phone !!

New Levels of Thinking
"The world
we have created today
has problems
which cannot be solved
by thinking
the way we thought
when we created them."
· *Albert Einstein*

37

Tip!
Keep a phone log. Record the time when a call came in, who it was, the company, phone number, topic, actions agreed to or asked for, and how long you talked. Periodically go back and analyze your calling patterns and the patterns of people who call you. You'll make some surprising discoveries that you can use. I discovered that I had three clients with whom I regularly worked who, if I called them after 5:00 P.M. on a Friday, were always there, always answered their phones, and always gave me new ideas or insights.

study patterns in your phone calls

LEVEL 2 TOOL #5: E-MAIL

Even more efficient than voice mail is E-mail. You can wait a long time to reply, really think through the reply, play with it before you send it, and keep a written record of your "conversations." You can also "copy" other people on the message. For the same reasons, think about your thinking and be aware of (not careful of) what you're writing.

To think about Level 2 changes in action, consider the military term "standard operating procedure" and visualize an F-14 fighter getting ready to take off from an aircraft carrier. Everyone is in place and acting in sequence. The choreography must be perfect. The aircraft is cocked and ready. Brakes are on. The crew is off to the side, having checked everything. Signals are given to the pilot in the cockpit. The catapult engages, the crew moves back and kneels down out of the blast. It all happens like clockwork. The same way every time. This is Level 2—all the right things being done right. Or so it seems.

Actually, a scene like that is one of the most creative and innovative I can think of. No two carrier launches are the same, and no two recoveries—carrier landings—are the same. Things start out right, being done right. Then little things go differently, or sometimes even wrong. At that point all Level 1 and 2 stuff goes by the wayside. The crew has to think, think fast, and think very creatively. They suddenly have a situation that is real different, Level 6 change, or worse, Level 7 change—"this can't be happening!" They

38

innovate on the fly—they come up with ideas they've never had before, and they implement them almost as they're thinking them, building on the right things (Level 1 and Level 2 training) and hoping they'll work. They usually do. Think back to this when we get to Level 6 *Different*…

MINDSHIFT
Level 2:

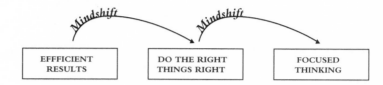

EFFFICIENT RESULTS	DO THE RIGHT THINGS RIGHT	FOCUSED THINKING

The above diagram illustrates the mindshifts necessary to do the right things right. You have to focus on the right things before doing things right will achieve efficient results. Focusing on the right things keeps you from doing the wrong things right—a not particularly useful thing to be doing.

PROS & CONS
Level 2 thinking and doing is almost second nature to people. It's part and parcel of succeeding, not just in business but in your personal life as well. The results and payoffs from Level 2 changes show up quickly in energy, money, and time, leveraged even further today by technology—a huge positive change force in our lives.

The drawback is that Level 2 thinking can lead to stagnation of ideas. In the extreme, it can become reflexive, non-thinking, operating by rote. If you have a highly efficient operation, and everyone is simply doing what is known to be the most efficient way to operate, they don't have to think. All they have to do is do.

Efficiency can be one of the biggest blocks to transitioning to any other level of change. When you are operating at Level

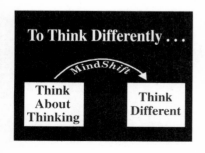

1 and Level 2 simultaneously, you are highly competent, so there is a tremendously strong bias against change. Why would you want to become less competent? "If it ain't broke . . . " A preoccupation with Level 2 can create a sense of urgency that totally overshadows what is really important.

ROLF'S THEORY OF RELATIVITY

Level 2 is far more definite than relative. Americans are so biased toward saving time and working efficiently that when I talk about saving time and effort and resources as doing the right thing right, people connect immediately. Time is money in most businesses. Time is precious in most families. Somehow there just isn't enough of it. We all want more of it. The Kirton Adaption-Innovation scores (see Getting Ready for Change) of almost every group we've ever worked with are biased heavily toward the adaptive side of the Efficiency subscale. Efficiency is an underlying component of the majority of ideas at every level of change.

When you can do things simultaneously at Level 1 and Level 2, you are competent.

THINKING ABOUT THINKING

Level 2 thinking is efficient thinking—thinking or producing ideas with a minimum of waste, expense, and unnecessary effort. Level 2 thinking exhibits a high ratio of output to input, meaning a lot of ideas from a little thinking. Level 2 thinking has an almost automatic aspect to it; it's J.I.T. thinking—Just In Time.

Level 2 thinking is seamless, almost nonthinking. Rock climbing comes to mind for me at Level 2. When you are rock climbing, you are thinking about trying to keep your weight balanced over your toes and feet so that your hands are free to move smoothly over the rock to steady yourself and explore future moves. You try to conserve energy in movement and effort. When you make a move, you focus on doing the right things right, efficiently, over and over, until you get to the top—if you can.

40

BIG Tip!
Me, Inc. is profound
stuff — Take the
time to do it.

what's my mission?
— my purpose?

ME, INC.®

The Me, Inc.® exercise at Level 2 is not about efficiency; rather, it's about the underlying concept of Level 2: doing the right things right. This exercise helps you define your strengths and skills. Think about what you do well, what you are best at, what you do better or differently than those around you—the right things that you really do right. Think about the compliments people pay you. Consider the basic qualities you have available. With this list in mind, try to define your basic mission. Make a rough cut, then come back later and refine it. Remember, you are thinking about what your purpose is in life—what your focus is—how you do the right things right. Go back and connect this with what you did at Level 1 on your Me, Inc.®

TRANSITION TO LEVEL 3

Level 3 is about moving beyond competency. When you are effective and efficient, and you can simultaneously do the right things and do the right things right. Focus your thinking and practice J.I.T. thinking. You know the process and procedures—then things go wrong—you have to move to a higher level. Level 3 is about improving. To improve, you have to move away from the minutiae and look at the big picture, the connective processes.

But you don't leave Level 1 and 2 thinking behind. While climbing through the 7 Levels of Change, as changes are implemented, you return to Levels 1 and 2, redefining what is right and then perfecting it. When you move to performing and thinking and operating at Level 1 and Level 2 change simultaneously, you've become fully competent, and then you can focus on doing things better—becoming *more* competent.

Level 3 is about better.

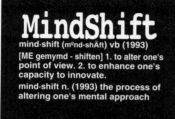

MindShift
mind·shift (mºnd-shÄft) vb (1993)
[ME gemymd - shiften] 1. to alter one's point of view. 2. to enhance one's capacity to innovate.
mind·shift n. (1993) the process of altering one's mental approach

Levels of Change

LEVEL 7: Breakthrough-Doing things that can't be done
LEVEL 6: Different-Doing things that haven't been done before
LEVEL 5: Adapting-Doing things other people are doing
LEVEL 4: Cutting-Doing away with things
LEVEL 3: Improving-Doing things better
LEVEL 2: Efficiency-Doing things right
LEVEL 1: Effectiveness-Doing the right things

41

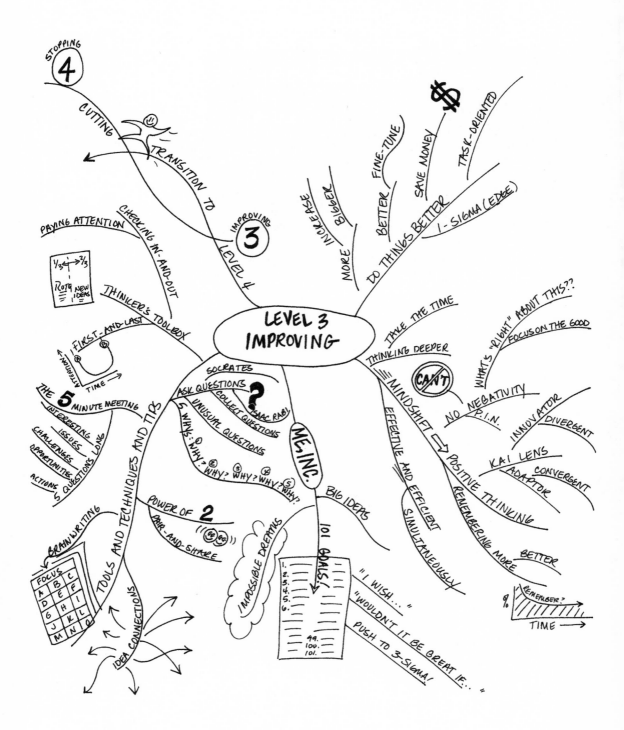

LEVEL 3: IMPROVING

DOING THINGS BETTER

UNDERSTANDING LEVEL 3

There are three key words that immediately let you know you are thinking, doing, or changing at Level 3: more, better, and improve. Changes at Level 3 involve fine-tuning, ways to speed things up, shorten delivery time, increase functionality, or reduce downtime. Level 3 change makes something more effective, more efficient, more productive, more valuable. At this level, "better" is a constant theme.

Continuing with the analogy of moving into a new job, once you've made enough personal Level 1 and Level 2 changes to be comfortable in the job, when you are truly effective and efficient, you are essentially competent. You know <u>what</u> the job is (Level 1), and you understand <u>how</u> to do it (Level 2).

When you can do the right things and do them right, you can begin to focus on ways to improve your core activities—fine-tune them to make them better—how to simultaneously make them more effective and more efficient.

People operating at Level 3 are still pretty focused and task oriented. Like Level 2 thinkers, they will be less inclined to look at the big picture and be more inclined to come up with ways to improve specific processes, particularly saving time and money.

Level 3 thinkers are not as rule oriented as Level 1 and 2 thinkers. They are still likely to be neat and organized, but they aren't quite as "by the book." They've learned "the book" and know it well, and they continuously see ways to make it better—and how to use it better. If they have finished their job and done it well, they may leave the office early. If it takes all night, they'll be there to get it done, but you can bet that they'll analyze the situation that led to the late night and figure out how to do it better the next time.

An interesting instance of exactly that is something that led to a major bottom-line difference for Kentucky Fried Chicken in New Zealand. Nick Sealey, the KFC marketing manager in New Zealand, began to notice something interesting. Customers would get in the queue to buy a meal during a peak business period, wait a few minutes, and then leave without buying anything—they'd go buy somewhere else. When he asked them about it, they'd say, "We love the taste, but the queue isn't worth it."

44

Nick was going to have to improve service, do better than a two-minute wait to place an order and a twelve-minute wait for a meal, since KFC was losing 15 percent of its customers. Nick organized some teams, focused simultaneously on improving effectiveness and efficiency, and improved service significantly: one-minute maximum to place an order and no more than a five-minute wait for the meal. Results: a turnaround 25 percent increase in sales with no advertising, just better (faster) service.

THINKING ABOUT THINKING

The thinking needed at Level 3 is better thinking—thinking that is higher in quality than other thinking. It is thinking that is more useful, suitable, or desirable than thinking that is simply efficient or focused. It's positive thinking—thinking that moves things forward in the direction of progress. It is thinking that is unencumbered by negativity or the tendency to criticize ideas. Level 3 thinking is "normal" but beginning to push the edge of the 1–Sigma range. It's about learning to think efficiently and effectively simultaneously. It's about taking time to think and it's about thinking deeply. Level 3 thinking is thinking to understand, learning how to actually listen to other people's ideas, and thinking about what they said. It's probing—thinking about the thinking behind your own and other people's thinking.

MINDSHIFT

Level 1:

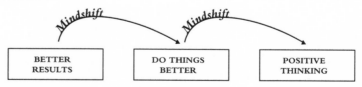

| BETTER RESULTS | DO THINGS BETTER | POSITIVE THINKING |

Level 3 thinking starts by reflecting on your thinking, and asking yourself: "In what way might I think better?" The mindshift needed for Level 3 thinking focuses on better from a positive angle—not by trying to figure out what's

Mindshift is about *CHANGE!*

wrong with something but, rather, what's right—and how it could be made even better. To get better results, you have to do things better. To do things better, you have to think better. So the first Level 3 challenge you face is how to think better.

Much of our thinking is governed by what we remember. Remembering provides a baseline for our thoughts and ideas to draw from and build on. Unfortunately, people don't remember things very well because they don't remember much of what they hear very long. After listening to a talk or presentation or conversation, the short three- to five-minute period immediately afterward is the time when your retention is close to 100 percent. That doesn't last long. Within an hour it has dropped to about 30 percent. By the next day it's down to about 10 percent, and after that, it gradually dwindles to almost nothing.

And what do we do? At the end of a class or a talk, we immediately get up and leave, blowing the three- to five-minute window of near 100 percent retention.

Studies have shown, and smart students know, that the first and last things said in a conversation or presentation or class are remembered best. The old wisdom to speech makers builds on this. "Tell 'em what you're going to tell 'em (first

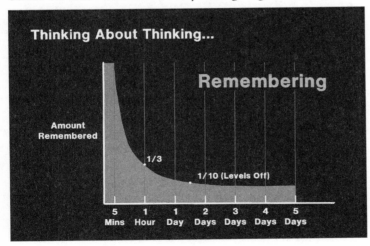

Thinking About Thinking...

Remembering

Amount Remembered

1/3

1/10 (Levels Off)

| 5 Mins | 1 Hour | 1 Day | 2 Days | 3 Days | 4 Days | 5 Days |

46

thing), tell 'em, and then tell 'em what you told 'em (last thing)." Students quickly learn to check out during the "tell 'em" part and check back in at the wrap-up.

Finally, consider the fact people don't pay attention to other people very long. People mentally begin to check out of the process of listening after a relatively short time—fifteen to twenty seconds—and begin to think about or focus on something else. They check back in when the subject changes, when it's their turn, there's a pause, or when something new catches their mind. They operate the rest of the time in a state of in-and-out listening.

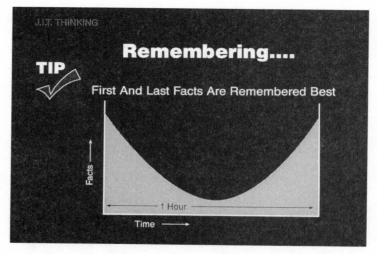

So, how do we use all this? Instead of beating people up for not remembering, for not listening, and for not paying attention, encourage them to do it. They're going to do that anyway. But then show them how they can use those facts to remember a lot more and think a lot better as a result. Here are some tools and techniques to help you do that:

LEVEL 3 TOOL #1: THE THINKER'S TOOLBOX

This is a J.I.T., Just In Time, thinking technique that can significantly improve both your retention of information and your ability to make idea connections. It builds on remembering right away firsts and lasts, and it leverages in-and-out

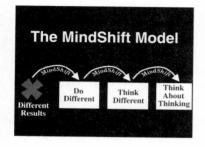

47

listening. Different people have different cycles and patterns of listening and paying attention. The key is to capitalize on that. By becoming aware of the fact that you check in and out while you're listening and having a feel for what your own cycle of listening or attention span is, you can increase your retention. When you feel your attention wandering, deliberately check out and begin writing down the new thoughts that are coming to mind, whatever they may be. After doing that, your mind is uncluttered, and you can much more easily check back in and reconnect to what is going on in your meeting or seminar or lecture.

The toolbox itself is simple to make. Simply draw a line down a regular 8 ½ by 11-inch sheet of note paper, dividing it into two sections lengthwise (⅓ and ⅔). The left-hand side, the ⅓, is for making rote learning notes while you are paying attention. Not sentences, but notes—key words and short phrases—chunks of information that capture the essence of the subject at hand. By leaving the right ⅔ of the paper open, you leave room for future idea connections and other thoughts. Most note-takers don't plan ahead like this for lateral thinking. It's an improvement to the more typical way of taking notes.

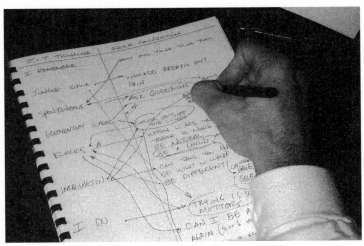

48

As your attention wanes, and you feel yourself checking out, move over to the right-hand side of the paper and write down whatever you are thinking about now. Draw on other things you know. When you do that, you are creating new knowledge—connecting your wider knowledge to what you've just heard. Try moving back to the left-hand side and reflect on what you didn't write down. Then try to make connections between what's missing, other information you already know or have previously learned, or perhaps connections between several different ideas you've already written down on the left-hand side of your paper.

Reinforce your connections by drawing arrows or lines to connect your thoughts on the left and right sides. This visual emphasis increases your ability to remember information.

LEVEL 3 TOOL #2: THE THINKER'S POSITION

When you complete a class, talk, session, or meeting, go into a J.I.T.—Just In Time think. "Assume the position"—lean forward, elbow on your knee or table, chin in your writing hand—and for three minutes reflect on the notes you've taken and the idea connections on your Thinker's Toolbox without writing or adding to them. Then write down three new thoughts or ideas beyond your notes. This simple habit can nearly double your retention of material covered.

Another way to mindshift to better thinking is with questions. Thinking is inspired by questions, both in the person questioned and in the questioner. Isaac Isador Rabi, Nobel Prize winner in atomic and molecular physics and holder of an amazing string of scientific honors, was once interviewed about how he had come to be who he was. A good son, he attributed it to his mother. He said that as a child, when he would come home from school his mother, Jennie Teig Rabi, would greet him the same way every day:

"Did you ask any good questions today, Isaac?"

Her perpetual question forced him to continually think about questions, develop a questioning attitude, and ask questions in school. A good question can be irritating—it

Results are about CHANGE!

forces people to take time to think! Questions take time. They make us pause and reflect and think about what we are doing. "The important thing," said Einstein, "is never to stop asking questions."

The average child asks 125 probing questions a day. The average adult asks six. All too soon, children learn to stop asking questions that Mommy and Daddy can't answer. The same thing happens later in school with teachers. In fact, in school we learn answers to questions we never asked or were going to ask. The end result is we begin to shy away from questions and lose what was once innate curiosity and inquisitiveness. Yet, questions are the primary way we learn.

The great Greek thinker and philosopher Socrates taught by asking questions, and through his questions, directed the focus of his students' thinking, making them come up with their own answers. The Socratic method can be relearned today as a tool for better thinking.

Did you ask any good questions today...??

LEVEL 3 TOOL #3: GOOD QUESTIONS

Start collecting questions. When someone asks a good question, or one that's particularly thought provoking and causes you to become thoughtful and reflective, write it down on a Blue Slip (and tell them that's what you're doing, that you collect great questions). Develop a set of interesting and stimulating questions.

Pick a favorite question and begin asking it of people in places where you don't normally ask questions. Practice with it for a while at home with your family or at conferences and meetings.

For instance, two of my favorites are:

"What's something you don't know?"

"What's a thought you've never thought before?"

Also, there are some great "starter" phrases from the Creative Education Foundation's Creative Problem Solving (CPS) technique that you can use to turn any challenge or issue into powerful questions:

"In what way might we—"

50

"Wouldn't it be great if—"

Then you follow those with: "What has to happen for that to happen?" And you're on the way to some pretty creative and better thinking.

LEVEL 3 TOOL #4: QUESTION TRACKING

Start keeping track of any questions you notice that you ask habitually, the questions you are most comfortable with. These are the questions that direct your focus, and, surprisingly, they direct how you think and how you feel. Notice and think about the kinds of answers they generate, and how those answers affect the quality and focus of your thinking—and through your thinking, your life. (This is also an important technique to use with your Me, Inc.® process.)

LEVEL 3 TOOL #5: THE FIVE WHYS

Learn to ask "Why?" again. As little children we asked "Why?" a lot. That powerful tool for better thinking was gradually lobotomized out of us because it pushes people's thinking so hard. Parents and teachers reach a point of frustration having to answer all those questions. They take time, and sometimes they don't have the answers.

Today, as part of the quality and continuous improvement process in many companies, employees are being retaught to ask "Why?" five times. In root cause analysis processes, the Five Whys technique essentially peels back the covering on a problem like the layers of an onion to eventually expose the underlying cause. The first "Why is that?" is usually pretty easy to answer. The second "Why is that?" about the first answer pushes the thinking deeper. The third "Why is that?" pushes the answer to the edge of 1-Sigma, the edge of normal answers. By the fourth "Why is that?" people are really thinking (and getting irritated, too!), and you begin to approach the real root of things. The fifth "Why is that?" pushes the answer well into 2-Sigma thinking, and usually it's enough to reach the level of root cause in a problem area.

Mark James was a young British engineer I met in Thousand Oaks, California. He had been assigned to

LEVEL 1
Effective

Doing the Right Things

51

Exxon's Western Production Division for a three-year, career-broadening assignment. But this was Southern California! What could a Brit know about the oil business in Southern California (despite the fact that Mark had been in international oil production operations all over the world)? So he didn't get a real job. Instead, Mark was told his job was to "go make money." Roam around, ask questions, learn things, and "make money." Mark took it seriously. He began to use the Five-Why probe—"Why? Why? Why? Why? Why?"— to dig into things deeper. "Why are we doing this?" or "Why is that?" and "Look, I'm just a simple Englishman. Why do you do this that way?" Then he'd come back with an idea. At first he would get hit on the head and beaten up badly by old thinking. Then he would come back again with another idea or a solution to a challenge. For every three or four ideas of his, one might work. He was quite an idea-generator with a pretty high Kirton Adaption-Innovation score. In his short three years he personally accounted for well over $10 million in savings and cost reductions for Exxon. Pretty soon, when Mark talked, people listened. He prompted an important mindshift: "—maybe some of these ideas might work."

There is a point at which you need to stop asking questions in order to make progress to change things. Questions are about Level 3 Thinking. If you keep asking questions, you'll continue to be uncertain, and only *doing* things will produce change. At some point you have to stop questioning and thinking and start doing. The questions at that point are: "What action could I take now to get started? What can I *do*?"

Consider meetings. People hate meetings. They churn and churn without doing anything. And meetings have been shown to eat up more time than any other single thing in business. An effectively and efficiently run meeting is a real anomaly. If you can build a better meeting, not a better mousetrap, the world will beat a path to your door. Wouldn't it be great if…we could run a meeting in five minutes? The better meeting!

*why? ? the 5 why's
why? ?
why? ?
why? ?
why?*

52

LEVEL 3 TOOL #6: THE FIVE-MINUTE MEETING

This is a powerful tool to save time and get people focused fast. By it's design, it is simple, effective (Level 1 change), diff*erent* (Level 6 change), and for most people very efficient (Level 2 change). So it really connects well for people subconsciously on the lower levels of change. But it really is a Level 3 change—it improves meetings significantly.

You can start a meeting with a Five-Minute Meeting, or you can insert a Five-Minute Meeting into the middle of a longer meeting that's dragging and get it refocused to be more effective and efficient, or you can end a meeting with a Five-Minute Meeting to sum it up.

The Five-Minute Meeting format is like no other meeting people have been in. There is no discussion, no rambling. The basic Five-Minute Meeting is designed as an "Interrupter" to be inserted in the middle of a bogged-down, boring meeting. Through the use of five questions combined with Blue Slips, this very structured process stimulates thinking, energy, and engagement, and promotes the generation of ideas and action. It builds on the premise that in any meeting, no matter how bad, some interesting ideas have been touched on. Also, there are some key issues and challenges either on the table or under the table, and buried in the interesting ideas, the issue, and the challenges, there is probably an opportunity. Finally, there is sure to be some action that needs to be taken no matter what else happens. It is on these basic contents of any meeting that the Five-Minute Meeting builds.

This process can be injected into a meeting at a pause or lull, when the discussion has gotten too heated, when one person is clearly dominating the discussion, when an agenda item has been covered and the group is ready to move on, or just before or after a break.

To insert a Five-Minute Meeting into an ongoing meeting, simply say, "We need to stop this and do something different!" Then hand out Blue Slips and explain how to use them. Ask everyone to write the word "INTERESTING" in the upper left-hand corner, focus their thinking on what's been covered

To Be Effective . . .

MindShift

Do The Right Things

Focused Thinking

so far in the meeting, and write down the most interesting idea or subject that's come up. Give them about 45 seconds to do this, and <u>don't</u> wait until everyone is finished. Then proceed, one question at a time, through these four questions (45 seconds each, and each on a separate Blue Slip):

- What are the most crucial ISSUES facing us?
- What are the most pressing CHALLENGES facing you personally?
- What OPPORTUNITIES do these ideas, issues, and challenges present?
- What ACTIONS can we take now?

I find it helpful to give people the definition of "issue" and "challenge" and to highlight the differences between them as I ask the questions.

> ISSUE: Something out of your control or beyond your ability to change and which strongly impacts on an undertaking in which you are engaged.
>
> CHALLENGE: A difficulty in a job or undertaking but within your control or influence to take on or change.
>
> Income tax is an issue for most of us. It's out of our control. The challenge it creates is how to creatively report income and pay the actual tax.

To use a Five-Minute Meeting at the beginning of the meeting, start by telling your group, "This is going to be different! We're going to think differently, do things differently, have different ideas, and get different results." Next hand out Blue Slips and explain how to use them. The questions are a little different if they come at the start of a meeting. The operative key word for a starting Five-Minute Meeting is "EXPECTATIONS." Ask the group to write the word "EXPECTATIONS" in the upper left-hand corner of their Blue Slip and write down what they are expecting out of today's meeting. If they have more than one expectation, they need to write each one on a separate Blue Slip.

Next have them write the key word "QUESTION" on a Blue Slip and ask them what questions they feel should be

Tip! How to start any meeting diffferent

54

covered in this meeting (this is the equivalent of ISSUES in the middle of a meeting). Again, subsequent questions go on separate Blue Slips. Then tell the group there will be three more questions and key words to think about and that they will have forty-five seconds to focus, think, and write about each one. Ask each question one at a time:

- What are the biggest CHALLENGES facing you personally?
- What OPPORTUNITIES do you see for us?
- What ACTIONS or DECISIONS should we take today?

Tip! How to recap and end a meeting

If you use a Five-Minute Meeting to end a meeting, your thrust is a little different. Essentially, you are recapping and trying to get something to happen as a result of the meeting. The Five-Minute Meeting questions are an excellent catalyst, but the emphasis is on "So what?"

- What INTERESTING new thinking and ideas surfaced today?
- Based on this meeting, what are the most critical ISSUES facing us?
- Similarly, what are the biggest CHALLENGES for you personally?
- What OPPORTUNITIES do you see for us?
- What ACTION STEPS can we take now—both near and long-term?

When you're using Blue Slips in a meeting, initiate the process by asking a question that causes the people in the meeting to think about responses. Limit the response time to forty-five to sixty seconds per question. This time period is deliberately short and will frustrate some people. But push on, and let them know it's okay if their idea isn't finished.

I developed the Five-Minute Meeting while I was in the air force. It was a mainstay of the Innovation Briefing we

THINKING ABOUT THINKING

Level 1 Change
Focused Thinking

fo·cus·ed (fΩ"kŌs"d) n., pl. 1. to cause to converge on or toward a central point; concentrate.

55

Issues and Challenges are strategic drivers for change

used with our units, other commands, and our customers all over the world. It also was a major feeder into our long-range planning. The issues and challenges it surfaced became the drivers and the strategic needs for the requirements process. When I began working with Exxon, I used it and taught it extensively with great success. One of my partners, Al Lewis, refined and perfected it—particularly the techniques for patterning and connecting the Blue Slips and converting them into a hard copy "Executive Summary Report" following the meeting.

There are many ways to use or process the ideas that come out of a Five-Minute Meeting. Pairing-and-Sharing, a tool that will be talked about next, is what makes the Five-Minute Meeting powerful in terms of raising a group's energy. It saves time and provides the opportunity for people to verbalize their ideas to other people, leading to new and different ideas. If you're unable to process them on the spot by using a chalkboard or flip chart or reading through them, promise that a typed summary of the Blue Slips will be distributed no later than the next day. Speed of turnaround is vital to create a feeling of importance and immediacy surrounding ideas.

LEVEL 3 TOOL #7: PAIR-AND-SHARE—
THE POWER OF TWO

This is a great way to leverage a Five-Minute Meeting, or it can be injected into meetings on its own to heighten the energy and creativity levels. The single largest jump an idea ever takes is with the changes that come the first time it is shared with another person (When Pairing-and-Sharing after a Five-Minute Meeting, begin with step 2).

Step 1. Begin by stopping the meeting and making everyone write down some key ideas that have come out in the meeting or perhaps concerns, points, questions, etc. Remember, one idea per Blue Slip.

Step 2. Ask everyone in the group to pair up and take turns reading and discussing the things they have written down. Each person is allowed only two minutes for sharing

56

their ideas; then it's the other person's turn. This works best if the facilitator keeps time.

Step 3. (optional) Next, the facilitator asks everyone to pair up with a second person. This time they are only to share what they learned from the previous person they paired with—leaving out their own ideas and thinking. Each person is allowed only one minute. Note: You don't work from the last person's Blue Slips—but from memory!

Step 4. (optional) Finally, everyone writes down one new insight or idea they got from the exercise to share with the whole group. This can be done immediately, or the Blue Slips can be word-processed and distributed later.

Technique:

Pairing-and-Sharing can be done almost anywhere, using whatever is available to write on—even a cocktail napkin. It's a great way to break up and liven up a long speech or to engage the entire audience at the end and lead into a lively Q&A discussion.

This was a technique that Don Mercer, the president of Mohawk Industries in Calhoun, Georgia, adopted and used very successfully with large groups of Mohawk's top dealers at the annual Dealers Conference. He and I teamed up and gave the dealers a kind of Huntley-Brinkley presentation on Thinking about Thinking and how to think differently in what we called "The President's Forum." Don billed me as the Mohawk "Mind Doctor" and started off by telling the dealers that I was going to help them learn how to think diffferent. I then taught them how to use Blue Slips, introduced the Five-Minute Meeting, focused it on their businesses, paired them up to share their issues and challenges, and handed off to Don. Don was a redheaded ball of energy with a wild and energetic style, who engaged the dealers in some pretty exciting and very lively discussions. They left the conference with a lot of new ideas, tools, and techniques. Mohawk gained some tremendous insight into real world issues and challenges facing their key customers. It was a pretty solid Level 3 change and improved a lot of things besides the conference.

✴TIP!

Become Aware of Ideas

57

One day Don pulled me off to the side and said: "Mind Doctor, we need results! Now that you have everyone writing down all these ideas, we have to get them to turn the ideas into results. I don't want one of those consultants who stands on the pier and yells at us to row harder. I want you to get in the boat with us and row! Find a manager, get involved with his problems and his people, work with them in getting some results. I also want you to coach some of our senior leaders on how to lead and think differently—and how to get results."

Among other things, this led to my working much more directly with Larry Perugini, vice president of manufacturing operations, and Robert Wages, manager of the Calhoun Spinning Mill. Calhoun was at that time at the bottom of the heap and ranked fourteenth out of all fourteen mills in performance numbers. Larry Perugini (who was Robert's boss), Al Lewis (my partner), and I designed and ran a pretty focused Think 101 workshop to teach basic out-of-the-box idea-finding tools, techniques, and processes to a select group of Robert Wages's people, all the way down to the first-line supervisors. We covered creative thinking style (the Kirton Adaption-Innovation Inventory), Blue Slips, Five-Minute Meetings, the Pair-and-Share process, and how to jump-start ideas into action—Level 1, 2, and 3 tools and techniques. Simultaneously, we created a one-day workshop we called "Results 101: How to get different results," which I'll talk about when I get into Level 6 change—Different.

"Results 101"
- using the 7 levels to get different results

Level 1, 2, and 3 changes: I attended and participated in several of Robert Wages's daily meetings, introduced the Five-Minute Meeting, and got his management team to look at all the meetings they attended or held each week and how to change them. We developed a J.I.T./Just In Time process for developing action plans to focus on implementing Blue Slip ideas, set measurable goals, and track progress to improve operations. Supervisors and their team leaders began using Blue Slips and the Pair-and-Share process to debrief at the end of each shift change. By the end of January (three months), Robert Wages had moved the

58

Calhoun mill's performance numbers to first place, and Robert left me a great voice mail in his long, North Georgia drawl: "We've gone from the bottom of the heap to the top of the heap, the view is terrific, and I'm going fishing." The Calhoun mill stayed up there in the 1, 2, and 3 position for quite a while. From a Mohawk Industries point of view, it was a Level 7 change—Impossible.

LEVEL 3 TOOL #8: BRAIN WRITING (IDEA CONNECTION)

Taking improved thinking in meetings further and making meetings even better, consider Brain Writing, a quiet and different kind of idea-finding process. Blue Slips are efficient but not as efficient as Brain Writing, a great way to get ideas connecting in large groups. It requires a form like the Idea Connections form shown here, but they can be hand-made on the spot with normal-sized paper.

Everyone starts with one Idea Connections form or sheet of paper, defines the problem or issue at hand from his or her own perspective, and then writes down three ideas or solutions. People trade papers. The next person reads the three ideas the previous person wrote on the form and then comes up with three more ideas. Then they pass the paper on, trade again and again, and in a short period of time, the group generates a huge amount of ideas. This process engages everyone much more quickly than "brainstorming" and is typically much more productive than either Blue Slips or brainstorming in a very short period of time. It creates a very level playing field for everyone. Quiet people tend to participate more, both slower and faster thinking people go at their own pace, people embarrassed to say their ideas out loud get involved, "experts" and senior people can't dominate the group, and the variety of ideas generated is much broader.

ROLF'S THEORY OF RELATIVITY

Level 3 is very relative and draws a lot of debate. What's an improvement to one person may be a Level 1 change to

On Expedition!

TIP!

**Notice everything.
Write it down!**

...use Blue Slips

IdeaConnections

A	B	C
D	E	F
G	H	I
J	K	L
M	N	O
P	Q	R

60

The Chapter on "getting ready for change" gives more detail on KAI Theory

Divergent Thinking

Levels 4, 5, 6, 7

Levels 1, 2, 3

Convergent Thinking

another, or a total disaster to someone else. Especially if the Level 3 improvement is very focused, it often overlooks how it interrelates to what's going on in the rest of the company. It could start a snowball effect that may or may not be seen as an improvement elsewhere as the change rolls out.

Level 3 is a good place to begin looking at your thinking through the lens of the Kirton Adaption-Innovation (KAI) inventory. The more "adaptive" thinker will tend to look at things convergently, will focus primarily on how to improve things, and will accept most problems as stated. This person will stay primarily at Levels 1, 2, and 3, with both thinking and doing. The more "innovative" thinker will tend to think more divergently, open things up and push beyond thinking about improvement and "better" to emphasize different instead. His or her thinking will primarily be at Levels 4, 5, 6, and 7, accomplishing Levels 1, 2, and 3 change by embedding them in or making them part of ideas and concepts at the higher levels of change.

PROS & CONS

The side effects—secondary changes—lead you directly to the positives and negatives of Level 3. The positive side of Level 3 changes is easily measurable in time or money savings, in more sales, improved products, better processes. The drawbacks usually show up quickly, too, when Level 3 changes haven't considered interrelatedness—the impact a change will make on the organization as a whole—and the potentially much bigger changes that come in behind a seemingly simple change.

ME, INC.®

Setting goals is the next step toward mentally incorporating. Goal setting begins as a Level 3 task with Level 3 changes aimed at improving yourself. In the School for Innovators, we incorporate an exercise called "101 Goals" into the Me, Inc.® process. It involves writing down 101 goals and wishes in one sitting before going to sleep! This turns out to be quite a stretch for most people. Coming up with twenty to thirty goals, about one full page of note paper, isn't too difficult. These are the normal, everyday kinds of goals most people have. To push on up to fifty to sixty goals, two pages' worth, is much more challenging and is where most people get stuck. They've reached the normal, 1-Sigma boundary of "normal" thinking.

The next wall people usually hit is at about seventy goals, after they've included the goals that followed from "wishes" and "wouldn't it be great if" thinking. To get over this wall, people shift into Level 4 (doing away with things and habits) and Level 5 (doing things other people are doing) and have transitioned their thinking into 2-Sigma or interesting thinking.

The final stretch moves into the area of impossible dreams, into things you could never really see yourself doing but would love to somehow be able to. These last fifteen to twenty goals really do become out-of-the-box wishes that, for the person writing them down, are pure 3-Sigma or different thinking.

TRANSITION TO LEVEL 4

While Levels 1, 2, and 3 are about focus—doing the right thing, doing it right, and finally doing it better—Level 4 is about refocus. Taking a look again. When you think you're doing something better, to get to the next level of change, you must refocus—look again. The most natural way to refocus is to begin cutting—looking at what you don't have to do. The operative question as we move from Level 3 improvements into Level 4 is "What can I stop doing?"

Push your thinking! Write out a list of 101 goals & wishes tonight

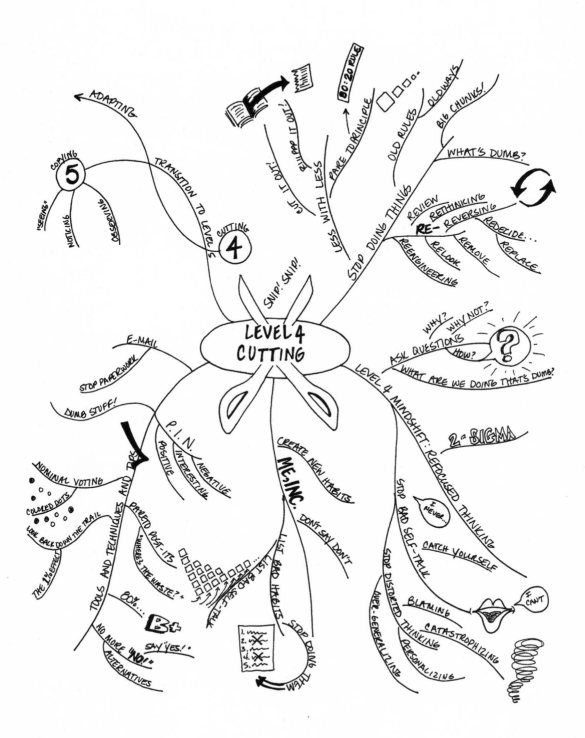

LEVEL 4: CUTTING

UNDERSTANDING LEVEL 4

Level 4 changes are about getting better than better. If you are effective and efficient, and improving and doing things better, you can make large-scale improvements by moving to Level 4 and begin to cut out things you don't need to do.

Here—where you are doing away with things or stopping doing things—the payoff is incredibly high.

Everything you do at Level 4 is based on the Pareto Principle—known as the 80:20 rule. From the Italian economist Pareto, we learn that 80 percent of the value in your productivity comes from 20 percent of your effort. So, it follows, you can cut out the other 80 percent and do more with less. Reset your focus. Develop a Pareto mind-set. Concentrate on the 20 percent and let the other 80 percent slide for a 4:1 return on your efforts.

To accomplish this type of cutting, you first have to look for the 20 percent that is creating the higher yield. Taking Pareto to the next order, applying it twice, you can get extremely focused: 20 percent of the 20 percent (or 4 percent) accounts for 80 percent of the 80 percent (or 64 percent) of the value—the 64:4 rule. So, to really leverage yourself,

refocus your efforts by concentrating on the 4 percent for a 16:1 return. Figure out where your 4 percent is and focus on it with a vengeance. Farm out the bottom 64 percent you do. Hire other people to do it—or just walk away from it. On a grand scale, it's just not that important. That leaves 32 percent in between—things that you probably need to keep doing but not with as much effort.

People doing, thinking, and changing at Level 4 are more likely to be preoccupied with saving money than with saving time. They are less rule oriented, and, in fact, eliminating old rules and long-standing guidelines will likely be a recurring theme with them. Getting rid of rules opens things up to allow them to generate more ideas and find greater savings. This is where classic "out-of-the-box" thinking starts: Change the size of the box by getting rid of rules and customs that define its edges.

LEVEL 4 TOOL #1: PIN

Eighty percent of new ideas don't get implemented because they are shot down by negative thinking. They are NIPped in the bud. Reverse your thinking and try

64

Tip! P.I.N. is a powerful mindshifting Tool

the PIN approach instead to make sure ideas get a chance to develop.

P—first, find something *positive* about a new idea.

I—next, find something *interesting* about it.

N—last, look for the *negatives.*

By suspending judgment, you are cutting out the negative thinking that stops creativity and idea flow.

My family has achieved some amazing savings with some Level 4 changes. We live in Houston, reported to be the most air-conditioned city in the world. I offered to pay my two youngest daughters, Amanda and Amy, half of the savings on the electric bill each month if they would just turn the lights out when we leave the house and turn the air-conditioning down when it isn't needed. My wife Julie, when she heard me, wanted a piece of the action, too. Since 1992, when we started this practice, the air-conditioning in our house has run only when the temperatures are in the high 90s. Even then we only use it long enough to bring down the temperature in the house. The actual dollar savings, not just the percentage change in our monthly bills, are amazing. Julie took that Level 4 change one step further. She used her piece of the action to lease a horse for a year, and, looking at how often we would actually be able to ride him, cut the costs by only leasing half a horse (that is, half the days available for riding).

Another easy step to personal cutting is to ask yourself: "If I had to live with 10 percent less income, how could I do it without changing my lifestyle significantly?" What can you give up or stop doing? Consider what would happen if you put that 10 percent into a savings account or IRA or invested it somewhere it could grow or compound interest.

When you make this type of thinking a habit, it's easier to get your employees thinking this way, too. Imagine how quickly the savings could grow if everyone in the company develops the habit of thinking of ways to cut.

On Thinking Expeditions, I use the example of John Keating (Robin Williams), the poetry teacher in the movie *Dead Poets Society,* telling his class to rip out the introduction

of their books. "Rip out the whole introduction...it's not the Bible. You're not going to go to hell for this," Keating says. Keating challenges his class to learn to think for themselves again. This scene is a powerful way to get people thinking about ripping out unnecessary steps, actions, and rules in their own lives.

Working with Hoechst Celanese Corporation on a project at its Bay City, Texas, chemical plant, I led a two-day Thinking Expedition built around the 7 Levels of Change to help a twenty-person team cut $2.4 billion out of the project budget and bring it in at $5 million. The project involved moving operations from a Bishop, Texas, plant and doing some new construction in Bay City. When we got to Level 4, we had a breakthrough. À la Robin Williams, we tore up the engineering drawings and threw them in the air. They were a big piece of the 80 percent—the high-cost items. Working with crayons and butcher paper, we re-engineered, only concentrating on the essentials. By cutting out major pieces of the contracted engineering process and instead doing it in-house, the cost of the project was eventually cut back to $4.6 million.

"The results were incredible," says Bill Cornman, engineering manager at Hoechst Celanese and sponsor of the Thinking Expedition. "I still can't believe it came together like that."

At Avery Dennison's research center in Pasadena, California, as a result of a Thinking Expedition, the process of all employees filling out work logs was stopped. Now only the managers fill out the log for their personnel, creating a time savings of twenty hours per month, 240 man-hours per year.

LEVEL 4 TOOL #2: E-MAIL

At Avery Dennison, 75 percent of the technical reports are now distributed by E-mail. Chemists have saved time spent in printing reports, making copies, and distributing them. Results: total savings of $1,600 a month in materials and labor. E-mail was mentioned in Level 2 as a straight efficiency change, but it also has incredible ability to cut across

Rippppp!! what could you Rip out?

normal hierarchical distribution lines and move an organization into network mode in terms of moving information. E-mail is also typically brief; a lot of nonvalue stuff has been cut out of it. Further, it eliminates huge amounts of paper and time spent at the copier producing the paper to send out through normal distribution to be filed and clog up the system. What areas of your organization can shift into E-mail and achieve a major Level 4 win?

On another Thinking Expedition, working with Exxon Corporation, our goal was to reduce the construction, operating, and maintenance costs on oil and gas field production facilities in Alaska. Working through Level 4, we identified building the access roads to the sites as an extremely high-cost item—$1 million a mile for an average of forty to fifty miles per site. The solution—don't build roads—cut them out completely! Consider instead alternative access technologies such as low-cost airlifting, all-terrain vehicles and sea approach amphibious access—concepts that heretofore would have been cost prohibitive. A very different look can now be taken at proposed new production site locations with the potential for multimillion-dollar savings.

LEVEL 4 TOOL #3: DUMB

People know where waste is. Get everyone in your company together and ask two straightforward questions: "What are we doing that's dumb?" and "What could we stop doing that no one would notice?" Try implementing just 10 percent of the ideas generated and measure and track the savings. Do less with less—not more with less!

LEVEL 4 TOOL #4: PARETO POST-ITS

Give everyone a pad of Post-it Notes. Ask them to write down the areas where they believe there's waste in the system—things they could stop doing. Group the Post-its on a flip chart by major categories. Then stack the Post-its into columns and voilà! You have a Pareto chart. Focus in on the specifics in the tallest column. Ask people to develop quick-and-dirty action steps that can be taken to eliminate the

AhHA!

Blue slips are a form of compulsive scribbling

waste in that column. Then do it! Start implementing the action steps. Track the results and measure the savings.

Cutting meeting time can be a very popular Level 4 change in any company. Making meetings fun is also an asset. Introduce the concept of "Nominal Voting" to your employees to achieve both.

LEVEL 4 TOOL #5: NOMINAL VOTING

Nominal Voting is a convenient, structured way to converge a large number of options down to a manageable few. The term "nominal" suggests that the process does not involve the typical group dynamics of discussion and consensus building. Instead, selection of the most important or popular ideas are first narrowed down with a relatively low level of interaction. Nominal Voting is especially effective when all or some of the group are new to each other, or if the group is working on highly controversial issues and challenges. Also, Nominal Voting can help refocus a group that gets stuck or is in disagreement or is being dominated by an "expert."

The supplies needed are stick-on colored dots—the transparent type work best—some flip charts, and PIN Thinking (Positive, Interesting, Negative).

Using brainstorming and suspending judgment (PIN), the group generates a list of problems, issues, ideas, or options that are visible to everyone on flip charts. Each item is numbered, and the participants are asked to vote on the items using a Blue Slip without any discussion. Just ask them to record the item number, not the full description of the item, on the Blue Slip. It's necessary to explain that this voting step helps avoid groupthink. That is, each person individually makes choices before sharing those priorities with the group. The votes can be cast in various schemes, but the two that seem to work best are:

Weighted Rank-Order Voting—This method is useful when there are a small number of options or when the group needs to come to focus upon just two or three items. Ask each person to select the top five preferred ideas and rank them in reverse order. The most preferred gets

68

five points and the least one point. Then the members place the values next to the corresponding number on the flip chart. In small groups, each member can call out the numbers, and the facilitator can record the values and complete the overall weighted voting tally.

Category Voting—This is a particularly useful method when there is a large number of items for the group to choose from. At the beginning, three criteria categories are established, such as "most urgent," "very important," and "important but can wait," or "I personally will commit to this," "I will help some others on this," and "This is BIG—I'll play in if management does, too." Each person is then asked to identify a specific number of items in each category. For example, with a list of sixty items, each person might be allowed to identify ten, e.g., two as most urgent, three as very important, and five as important but can wait. Again, it is important that the group first votes individually on Blue Slips before placing the dots to avoid groupthink.

Then, using color-coded dots, votes are placed on the appropriate items: red dots for urgent (two dots worth five points each); green dots for very important (three dots worth three points each); blue dots for important but can wait (five dots worth one point each). This technique is very visual—the color clusters really highlight where and how much energy there is around each idea. The facilitator can tally up the votes, although the concentration of colors pretty much does the job.

After the tally, the group discusses the patterns and their reactions to them. Those items at the top of the list are ready to be worked into action plans, or they can continue to be expanded and enhanced through the creative thinking process.

Remember, voting is done individually, but the voting tally needs to be a group effort. While this can be done verbally, as people call out their numbers or show hands as each item is called, getting people to stand up and record their own votes generates energy in the group. It also gives people the opportunity to interact during the process.

The group's goal is to reach decisions that best reflect the thinking of all group members, that is, finding ideas,

"What gets written down gets done!"

proposals, and options that are acceptable enough and have enough energy that all participants will be comfortable supporting them. The decisions may not be everyone's first priority, but everyone has had an opportunity to participate. Consensus does not mean that everyone agrees; it means that everyone is willing to live with the decision.

Tip!
As a rule, allow each participant a number of choices equal to one-third of the total number of items on the list—for instance, thirty-six items, twelve choices. This ensures that a number of the items will have critical mass in terms of numbers of dots on them. With shorter lists, use fewer choices; with longer lists, use a higher number.

Tip!
Just because you have used Nominal Voting to converge down to a few ideas does not mean that the other problems, issues, ideas, or options are not important and should not be addressed. The time and place was simply not this session with this group. Because of a natural inclination for a group to be more adaptive and conservative during convergence (i.e., to "NIP" ideas), those items that are eliminated are often the most novel and interesting and should be explored in more detail at a later date.

ROLF'S THEORY OF RELATIVITY

Level 4 isn't very relative. Cutting is the clearest of all of the levels of change. There is little debate as to whether or not you are cutting something out or stopping something. This concept is very clear-cut when compared to effectiveness, efficiency, improving, copying, different, and impossible. There is very little subjectivity about cutting, except when it comes to deciding whether or not cutting is the right thing to do. Cutting back on the workforce may save money, but ask the person whose job has been cut whether that's doing things right and you might get a different perspective.

70

THINKING ABOUT THINKING

The mindshift at Level 4 is into refocused thinking. It's thinking about a central concept or idea again. It's thinking one more time about something with greater intensity. It's asking yourself, "What can we stop doing? What can I stop doing?" To stop doing things you must refocus your thinking. You must stop thinking along specific, corresponding lines, stop thinking about things in the way you're used to thinking about them—in your normal, 1-Sigma thinking pattern.

Another important aspect of Level 4 thinking is to stop distorted thinking—blaming, mind reading, being right all the time, catastrophizing, personalizing, over-generalizing. Apply the Pareto Principle to your thinking and stop thinking about the things that don't matter. Focus where it counts.

Tip!
"Re": Rethink, reframe, restate, redecide, revisit, re-create, remove, rediscover, repay, reprint, reexplore, recapture, relook, refund, realign, recopy, remake, rewrite, reverse, redo, reform, rejoice!

Re-everything!

MINDSHIFT

Consider the following mindshift model to help you achieve Level 4 changes. To get better, you have to stop doing things. To stop doing things, you must refocus your thinking. To refocus, to stop doing things, you must start asking questions. Why? Why not?

Level 4 thinking moves you into 2-Sigma or interesting thinking. You're on your way to breakthrough thinking.

Mindshift		*Mindshift*	
LEVEL 4: CUTTING	→	STOP DOING THINGS	→ REFOCUSED THINKING

Effective

How can you be more effective?

...BLUE SLIP

LEVEL 4 PROS & CONS

When you stop doing things, the effects are often immediate and bigger. The payoff is higher, people take notice.

Personally, when you cut out bad habits, you can look better, feel better, live longer. The negative side of Level 4 changes is that, typically, you have to give up something that was enjoyable or at least comfortable, and often you have to learn something new, which is a negative to some people. Giving things up can be hard. It takes twenty-one days to form a new habit, and longer if you have to stop doing an old habit simultaneously.

Generally, Level 4 changes irritate people significantly. If you can't make them see the magic in PIN, suspending judgment, they can get pretty defensive—which translates into becoming critical and attacking the change you're trying to make. Another drawback to Level 4 changes and applying the Pareto Principle is that the 80 percent you are not concentrating on will suffer if it's not delegated to the right hands. There's a challenge to figuring out how much effort needs to be given to that 80 percent that is cut out.

LEVEL 4 TOOL #5: B+

"B+ing" is a way to handle the other 80 percent. It may only bring in 20 percent of the value on the bottom line, but it still has to be done. B+ is a respectable grade. However, it takes considerably less time, effort, and resources to achieve than an A+. Save the A+ effort for the 20 percent that yields 80 percent of the bottom line. Statistically, everything cannot be A+. It's relative. Things follow the normal curve, and only a very small percentage can be A+. If you can achieve A+ on 20 percent of what you do, you will have skewed the normal curve significantly.

The concept of "B+" is a mindshifter!

ME, INC.®

Your Me, Inc.® exercise for Level 4 is to take ten minutes and make a list of all of your bad habits—things you want to stop doing. Then, pick the one you think or feel may be the easiest one to change and make a list of when it is you fall into that habit. Then begin to focus on the event that most often is connected with that habit. For instance, if you want to give up smoking, and you *always* [a word that clues you in to the

72

Don't try to stop every thing—all of something—at once

habit] light up a cigarette with your first cup of coffee in the morning, focus on stopping that specifically. Begin to notice every time you don't do it. At the end of each day, pat yourself on the back for not doing it. When you've truly broken that particular connection, go on to the next strongest connection or event of your habit. Cut out habits in small steps with Level 2 thinking. Use Level 2 changes to more efficiently make Level 4 work!

Tip!
It's easiest to stop an old habit by replacing it with a new, better habit. The new habit then begins to steal time away from the old habit gradually, and the old habit atrophies.

LEVEL 4 TOOL #6: LOOK BACK DOWN THE TRAIL
Periodically look back over your shoulder and make a list of everything you've stopped doing since the last time you looked. This can be a real boost. Stopping bad habits often feels like a much greater level of change than achieving a new goal that you once deemed impossible. Try it right now: Since the last time you thought about it, what have you stopped doing? Make a quick list and then go brag about it to someone!

LEVEL 4 TOOL #7: NO MORE "NO!"
One of the most important things you can do for yourself and your family is to get out of the negative zone and into the positive zone. Look for the positive. Start by trying to avoid saying "No!" Practice at home with your kids. Instead of saying, "No, you can't go outside and play" say, "Yes, later—after you do your homework" or say, "Give me a minute to think about it" or "Convince me." (Followed perhaps by, "I'm not convinced. Convince me.")   I got these tips from Barbara Colorosa who runs a great program called "Kids Are Worth It"—it works!

LEVEL 2
Efficient

Doing Things Right

LEVEL 4 TOOL #8: RIIIIPPPP OUT NEGATIVE SELF-TALK

Get rid of your "I can't…I always…I never…I hate…I'm no good with…" Catch yourself in negative self-talk and make a note of what you say to yourself—actually write it down. You'll soon discover that you have some real patterns, regular phrases you fall into. I remember very clearly when the power of negative self-talk really hit me. I was getting out of my car, already running late for a meeting, and dropped the papers I was carrying in a puddle next to the car. Flailing to catch them as they fell, I hit my head on the car door, slammed the door on my coat, and ripped it as I tried to walk away. "This is not going to be a good day!" I said out loud. And BAM! It hit me. I was setting myself up for more of what I'd just experienced. Now, when I catch myself moving toward bad self-talk, I instantly flash back to that moment on the corner of Bell and Louisiana in downtown Houston. Engage your family in this—make it fun. Sensitize everyone to the concept of bad self-talk and start catching each other in it. "Whoops! Dad—that's bad self-talk."

TRANSITION TO LEVEL 5

With Level 4, you've transitioned into 2-Sigma, interesting. You've cut away what's unimportant, and by doing this, there may be some holes you can fill in. Here you begin to move into Level 5—copying. One of the easiest ways to leap forward into clear innovation is by opening your eyes, to begin noticing what others do better or differently than you are doing, and copy and adapt some of it for your own use.

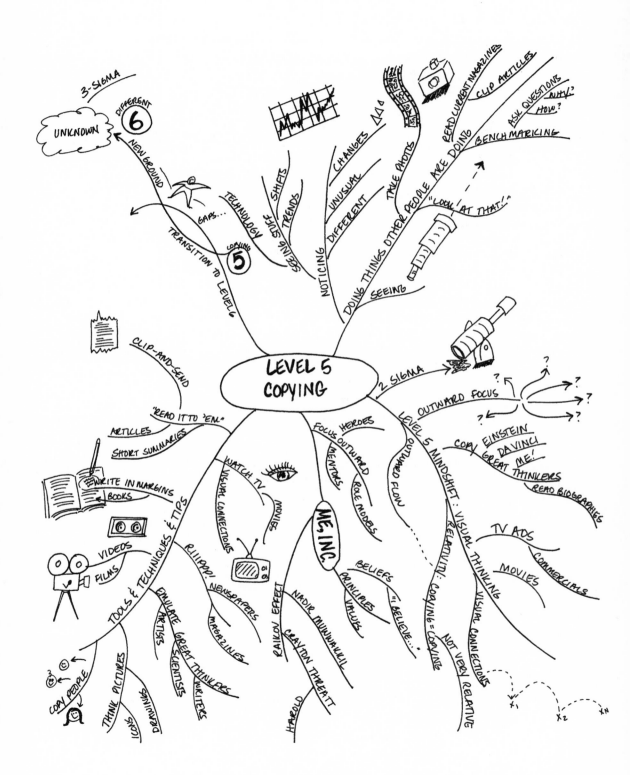

LEVEL 5: COPYING

UNDERSTANDING LEVEL 5

Almost by definition, Level 5 (Copying) doing and thinking is out-of-the-box. You look over and notice something that someone else—a company, a group, a person—is doing. And you think, "Hey, I could do that!" Then you copy what they are doing—only you don't do it quite the same way. Not exactly. You adapt it to your unique style or situation.

Noticing things is the fundamental thinking process behind Level 5 (Copying) changes. No matter what you call it, whether it's copying, learning from, benchmarking, or even reverse engineering, what you notice and then make into a Level 5 (Copying) change can dramatically kick-start innovation and at significantly lower costs in terms of time, resources, and effort. When you copy and adapt, you don't have to start from scratch, so it's possible to master an existing large-scale, complex process or even an entire system with the same level of effort it takes to implement a much smaller change.

Essentially, all of the hard parts are done: design, engineering, development, testing, and selling of the idea. Something that is being copied already works. It is a proven, fielded, operational concept.

Though we all learned early on in school that copying was not the right thing to do, "benchmarking," a process legitimized by the quality movement in corporate America, has given copying new status. In 1989, Robert Camp wrote *Benchmarking: The Search for Industry Best Practices That Lead to Superior Performance*. This was the first really prescriptive book on how to benchmark, and following its publication, companies began to look at their competitors in a whole new way—as fertile ground for ideas.

Benchmarking how other organizations do things (regardless of whether they are in your industry) and enhancing those discoveries and achievements (using Level 3, improving, thinking) is the hallmark of a successful innovator. Benchmarking helps you leap past the first four levels of change, which later come into play after an idea has been copied. After being benchmarked, an idea can be made more effective (Level 1), more focused and efficient (Level 2), tuned up and improved (Level 3), and aspects of it that don't quite fit or apply to you or your situation can be cut out (Level 4).

Leaders in many companies are uncomfortable with this level of change in part because they are so inwardly focused that they are often not aware of what others are doing that's worth copying. When using the 7 Levels of Change as a model for brainstorming ideas, Level 5 (Copying) is a predictable point where idea finding stalls with executives. Business leaders in general simply are not very aware of what is going on outside their own company or industry:

"I don't even have time to watch TV. There's no way I'm going to have time to read stuff that doesn't relate to work." These are comments I hear all the time.

LEVEL 5 TOOL #1: READ IT FOR 'EM!

When you notice something, a trend or shift in the paper or in a magazine like *Fortune* or *Business Week*, in a new business book, on TV, or in a new movie, make a note of it! Then take a moment and summarize it briefly. If you can make a copy of it (article or book), attach the note to the copy and send it to the busy person with something like "Joe—this reminded me of a comment you made the other day about X. Looks like you were right! Thought you'd enjoy seeing this." 1. Limit the length of your note. 2. Limit the length of your summary to no more than a half page in BIG print. 3. Be selective—don't overdo reading for somebody else. This works!

With many companies, classic Not Invented Here (NIH) thinking leads to resistance to imitating something someone else is doing. Too often, as a direct result of NIH thinking, the wheel is reinvented. Japanese corporations, however, are longtime world leaders in adapting and creatively improving upon the products and processes of others, making the best of the best even better by synergistically combining thinking at Level 3 (Improving) with Level 5 (Copying).

The Level 5 thinker and doer wants to know why. Why do we do it this way? Why do we need this? Why do they do it differently? You'll recognize the Level 5 thinker by the stuff torn out of magazines and taped to the walls in his or her office. Bulletin boards are fertile ground for them to share ideas, cartoons, articles they find interesting. With Level 5

BIG Tip!
Easy to do.

TIP!
Doing things right saves time
- Faster
- Quicker
- Sooner
- J.I.T.

thinkers and doers, you will start seeing more piles and less files in the office. On casual days at the office, they'll tend to dress much more casually than the folks at Level 1 (Effectiveness) and 2 (Efficiency), who might take off their tie. Level 5 (Copying) people are good bridgers—they bridge the Level 6 (different) and 7 (Impossible) thinkers to the Level 1, 2, 3 (Improving), and 4 (Cutting) thinkers, who otherwise would have a hard time communicating. They can see the good in Level 6 and 7 ideas and at the same time bring them down to earth.

Level 5 people are curious. They are outwardly focused, constantly asking others if they've seen this or heard of that. As children, they loved show-and-tell day at school. They love New! They will drag out the end of meetings looking for ways to share all of the new ideas they have or to listen to what others have seen or heard that's new to them.

LEVEL 5 TOOL #2: WRITE IN BOOKS

If you can get in the habit of writing in books, making margin notes, or writing Blue Slips while you read books, you'll have fertile ground for copying now or later. Make it easy on yourself by circling, starring, underlining, or highlighting so you won't miss a great idea. The habit of NOT writing in books is an old and hard one to break. Emphasize it by telling your friends when you loan them a book, to write in it. Show them some of your marginalia and tell them that's the only condition under which you loan books—that they keep it up.

LEVEL 5 TOOL #3: LET TV BE YOUR GUIDE

Television is a great tool for getting ideas to copy. Watch it—especially commercials—with your mind and eyes and ears actively engaged to spot something that will connect with a problem. You'll be surprised what you can copy and adapt. Millions of dollars' worth of market research goes into those commercials. Try to figure out the thinking behind commercials and figure out where you can put it to use in your life at home or at work. In fact, get in the habit of recording great commercials, then watch them a number of times, looking for the thinking behind the thinking.

Try it! Right now—WRITE something in the margin of this book

78

Video to watch: Melanie Griffith in "Working Girl"

LEVEL 5 TOOL #4: TEAR OUT NEW IDEAS

Before you throw away or recycle all of those magazines and catalogs that come your way, flip through them looking for at least one great idea to copy and tear it out! Look for new products and think about the ideas behind them. How can you apply those ideas to what you do? Send torn-out stuff to your friends and coworkers or boss with a short note.

LEVEL 5 TOOL #5: MAKE VISUAL CONNECTIONS

If you get stuck looking for ideas or solutions, disconnect and try to reconnect visually. Look through a coffee table book with a lot of pictures, look through your vacation photos, look out the window. Start by looking at simple images and progress to more complicated ones. Look at each image or picture for about a minute, writing down any and all ideas that come to mind. Then return to the question or problem at hand with those ideas as a mindshift, a new point of view.

We all know how Level 5 (Copying) changes work. Think about your own family. Children learn almost everything to a certain point from copying or emulating their parents. Here's how you wash the dishes. Here's how you cut the grass. Here's how you talk. Here's how you relate to other people. Children copy everything, and, by their doing so, we take them from low levels of competence to relatively high levels very fast.

Large companies have mastered continuous innovation by seeing what others do well and acquiring it. When a company such as Exxon sees an excellent location for a gas station that happens to be owned by a competitor, Exxon often buys it and changes the sign. Similarly, you'll often see Exxon stations located next to Mr. Lube. Why? Exxon liked what it saw, acquired a major share of Mr. Lube, and now often pairs the operations, locating them next to each other. When that's the case, it's easy for the Exxon station to refer oil changes next door.

In New Zealand, Kentucky Fried Chicken and Pizza Hut, both members of Pepsico's fast-food family, realized that the kitchens in both restaurants were different but similar. What if—the different in each could be adapted to the other (Level

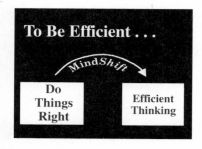

5 change—Copying), and the same could be combined and reduced (Level 4 change—Cutting), and it could all be done in a single KFC–Pizza Hut restaurant, a new hybrid (America's No. 3 motivator—BIG and more), with more choice (America's No. 1 motivator) and more efficiency (America's No. 4 motivator—time)? BAM! Done deal and going like gangbusters. Same kitchen, two different restaurant concepts, all under the same roof.

Pepsico had been dabbling in this for some time, but the idea hadn't gone anywhere. New Zealand KFC pulled together some folks, went through a Creative Problem Solving (CPS) process, came up with some completely different tangents (Level 6 change—different thinking), designed some new technologies (no rocket scientist stuff), and is now running the highest volume in the world for Dual Concept stores.

In the end, it was all mostly just common sense. They pulled people together, used a lot of School for Innovators processes, and actually started listening to people with an open-minded, "no bad ideas" approach. They didn't reinvent the wheel, they just changed the shape of it and adapted things other people were doing. They went out and carefully visited all their competitors who were doing "Gold Standard" things in service and products. Then they copied the competitors' best ideas (Level 5 copying) and adapted and improved (Level 3 change) them to fit KFC/Pizza Hut operations and concepts.

Their first big finding was that they couldn't service their consumer needs under the current restaurant design that they had. They pulled a team of staff and managers together, brainstormed, and used CPS to come up with a new breakthrough, flexible/adaptable floor plan (Level 6 Change—different).

They pulled together more teams from both KFC and Pizza Hut and had them each generate their ultimate vision for a restaurant (Level 7 thinking). Then they analyzed the concepts jointly, looked at what the similarities and differences were. Then they reversed roles and had the KFC gang design the Pizza Hut of the future, the Pizza Hut folks

80

design the KFC store of the future (Level 6 thinking/ doing—different). The result: some really great, different perspectives and ideas.

The old dual concept had two separate management teams, two sets of cooks under one roof, and never the twain would meet. The new KFC/Pizza Hut New Zealand concept moved to one management team, one staff team, and a lot of modification of standard ideas (Level 1 and 2 effectiveness and efficiency changes) based on staff input (Level 3 thinking: improvements). The big one was starting at the back of the restaurant where the very different raw materials come in, then progressively moving forward from the back, blending more and more of the functions and operations. To accomplish this, they modified a lot of the standard hardware (equipment, technology) and software (procedures, people skills). In the end, they were able to put the dual operation under one roof the same size as the traditional restaurant (Level 6 change—different!).

Exxon's Western Production Division's Innovation Center decided to hold a "little idea day" and discover what the biggest little idea might be. The biggest little idea came from a high school student. One of Exxon's engineers working on a project to cool gas coming in from an offshore platform, and under a pressing deadline to finalize the contract for the project with a contractor, was describing the problem and the construction of the project at the dinner table to his family. His son suddenly said, "Dad, why don't you just put in one of those big fans that blows over dripping water like (Level 5 copying) they use at the nursery to cool all the plants?" The family drove over to the nursery, looked at the setup, and the father went in and canceled the contract. A large fan was installed at a cost of $25,000 versus the contractor's proposed engineering design costs of $125,000.

ROLF'S THEORY OF RELATIVITY

The copying aspect of Level 5 is straightforward and easy to understand. However, the modifying and adapting

THINKING ABOUT THINKING

Level 2 Change

Efficient Thinking

ef·fi·cient (Ä-fÄsh"Önt) Adj. 1. Acting directly to produce an effect.

function of Level 5 can be very relative. If I copy something and put a twist on it, it can be viewed as only a Level 3 change because in one sense I am only improving. But if what I choose to copy was impossible for me before, I have jumped ahead to Level 7! As soon as I copy it, it is no longer a Level 7 idea. It can be viewed as different (Level 6) or improving (Level 3). Another aspect of the relativity of Level 5 is what people choose to copy and what that reveals about their own thinking. Some people will be more inclined to copy things that make an operation more effective and efficient (Levels 1 and 2), while others will look for what's different (Level 6) or impossible (Level 7).

THINKING ABOUT THINKING

Level 5 thinking is very visual thinking. To think at this level you have to see, perceive, notice, visualize. You have to use all of your senses and look for what's different, what's missing. Visual thinking is thinking that produces an image in your mind. It's imaginative thinking; it's possible thinking. As Yogi Berra once said, "You can really see a lot by observing."

Level 5 thinking is the highest level of 2–Sigma or interesting thinking. It raises mindfulness and noticing to an art form, seeing things with your mind in a different way. It's thinking that's flexible and responsive. Key words to thinking at this level are: see, notice, accommodate, shape, acclimate, adjust, transform.

MINDSHIFT

The more difficult side to Level 5 thinking is the mindshifts that go with it. There are two basic ways of thinking different to operate at Level 5. The first is to copy thinking that differs in style or type from your own, which can be a significant stretch. Studying and emulating the thinking processes and techniques of great thinkers can be a first step in shifting or changing your own thinking. Read the biographies of great and creative thinkers.

see, notice, accomodate, shape acclimate, adjust, transform

82

Tip!
Here are five excellent Level 5 books from which to copy great thinkers' thinking. The authors share a lot of stories and examples of style, techniques, habits, and patterns of thinking of people such as Einstein, Edison, Gauss, Curie, Mozart, Newton, Carver, Beethoven, and da Vinci.

> *The Einstein Factor*, by Win Wenger (1996)
> *Fire in the Crucible*, by John Briggs (1990)
> *Uncommon Genius*, by Denise Shekerjian (1990)
> *Secrets from Great Minds*, by John McMurphy (1991)
> *The Creative Process*, by Brewster Ghislin (1952)

The second way to operate at Level 5, seeing different, is a mindshift that first requires you to deliberately become more visual, to begin noticing things that are different and unusual when compared to the things you normally notice. It requires an opening up of your perspectives, horizons, and mental filters so that the noticing of different will come more easily.

LEVEL 5 TOOL #6: START LISTENING DIFFERENTLY
Keep your mind open and quiet and your mouth shut. Roll what people say around in your mind; play with it. Don't bog down in thinking about whether or not you agree or disagree with them, look for ideas in it. Paraphrase it back to them. Then pull out of what they said the stuff that works for you—copy or adapt it!

Consider the mindshift diagram below. In order to do things others are doing, you have to copy things. In order to copy them, you have to see and notice things.

Start carrying a camera all the time – take snap-shots of Ideas when they happen

Mindshift		*Mindshift*	
LEVEL 5: COPYING RESULTS		**DOING THINGS OTHERS ARE DOING**	**SEE AND NOTICE THINGS**

LEVEL 5 PROS & CONS
One of the pros to Level 5 is that it requires you to focus outward, a marked change from the first four Levels of

The Rules

KEYWORD

SHORT "IDEA"
TELEGRAPH STYLE

ISSUE:
How to get management to support this.

WRITE HORIZONTALLY,
NOT VERTICALLY

83

Change, which are very inwardly focused. Level 5 changes can be very easy and can jump-start innovation. Level 5 can accelerate your rate of change, compressing the time and energy needed to leap from Level 1 (effectiveness) to Level 7 (impossible)—just by opening your eyes to what others are doing well. Most great ideas already exist—go find them (apologies to George Pransky).

The downside to Level 5 thinking and doing is that it can get overfocused, isolating an idea that may not work in your own system the way it seemed to be working in the one you copied it from. Level 5 thinking also can stall your efforts at originality—it's not terribly creative to copy, and if you get in the habit, pushing your own internal envelope can atrophy, so Level 5 shouldn't be overused (credit to George Pransky).

ME, INC.®

As with the lower levels of thinking, doing and change, Me, Inc.® starts by focusing inward. This is an important process. Any change has to start with "me" before it can progress to "them." It's a little like conjugating a verb—from me to you to they. It's crucial to first become personally aware of a change in order to get others to buy into that change. At Level 5, Me, Inc.® begins to focus outward.

The Me, Inc.® exercise at Level 5 involves looking outward as you define your own principles and beliefs. Generally, your principles and beliefs start with the people around you—your family and friends. Your role models and mentors. Teachers, grandparents, authority figures. Americans believe in truth, justice, apple pie, and Mom. And when you grow up, that becomes part of your belief system (Level 5 change—copying).

As you continue to grow and mature in your thinking, you learn about others' beliefs and you think, "Gee, I believe that, too." And you copy and adapt some of them (Level 5 change) to fit you and your Me, Inc.® Level 5 thinking and doing connects with mentors and mentoring as well.

Think about your basic principles and beliefs. What are they, anyway? How do you govern your life? How have you changed how you operate? Have your principles and values

What are my basic operating principles??

84

and beliefs changed or shifted over time? How? Have some proved to hold solid over time? Have others fallen away?

One of the most amazing Level 5 changes I've ever seen took place during one of our School for Innovators in Estes Park, Colorado. Harold Crayton Threatt, then manager of quality for R. J. Reynolds R&D, was one of the students. Harold has a pretty strong Adapter KAI score (see Getting Ready for Change). His grandfather, Crayton Threatt, after whom Harold was named, had been a real innovator in his time. During one of the drawing-sketching exercises we use in the school, Harold drew a picture of the Harold side of himself reaching over and putting his hand over the mouth of the Crayton side of him every time the Crayton side came up with a good idea and tried to say something. At that point Harold decided to become his grandfather, Crayton Threatt, for the duration of the School for Innovators. Everything shifted! He stopped judging his ideas before they came out. He suspended judgment when he listened to other people. He tried things he'd never done before, and he became a deep thinker and risk taker almost overnight. He was a wonder to behold.

Without knowing it, Harold had stumbled onto the Raikov Effect. Dr. Vladimir Raikov, a Soviet psychiatrist, developed a deep hypnosis method, which he used to make people think they had actually become a great genius in history, such as Rembrandt or da Vinci. Raikov found that once they had "become" that genius, they took on the abilities the genius had been known to have had and were able to draw or paint or compose or play musical instruments with astounding ability and talent—demonstrating skills totally absent from their normal lives.

Harold Crayton Threatt transformed his own thinking without hypnosis—he simply took on all the remembered innovator traits of his grandfather (Level 5 thinking) and started living his life differently (Level 5 doing). He implemented much of his Me, Inc.® transformation on the spot in Colorado. When he returned to Winston-Salem, he changed his voice mail and now answers with "This is Harold Crayton Threatt." Today, if you want focus, convergence,

Efficiency is about TIME
- Quicker
- Faster
- Sooner

action, and a quick response, leave a message for Harold; if you want new ideas and out-of-the-box thinking, call and ask to speak with Crayton.

Tip! Copy Harold Crayton Threatt
If I have to explain this to you, you wouldn't understand.

TRANSITION TO LEVEL 6

The transition from Level 5 (copying and adapting) to Level 6 (diff*ferent*) is also a transition from 2-Sigma change to 3-Sigma change—a big leap.

Level 5 change and Level 5 thinking are built around noticing things, being able to see other people doing something, modeling something new. This level is built around copying the examples of others, using others' thinking *and* doing to inspire us.

Level 6 is diff*ferent*. At Level 6 (different), there is no one and nothing to copy. The essence of Level 6 is about doing things no one else is doing. Level 6 is about breaking new ground, leaving new trails and footprints for others to follow and to copy. Level 6 is not about same or consistency or order. It's about leadership—creating forward motion into the unknown. Just like making the leap from Level 3 (improving) to Level 4 (cutting), you can often transition from Level 5 (copying) to Level 6 (diff*ferent*) by taking a step back and looking for the gaps. What's missing? Where's there a niche that's not covered?

To understand diff*ferent*, to value different, to think and do different, is far easier if we can identify with it at the personal level—if we can personally connect it with ourselves. Think back to all the Me, Inc.® work you've done so far. How are you different? What makes you unique and special? What unusual experiences or adventures have you had? What have you done that no one else has done? What are some of the biggest changes you've ever personally experienced? On a relative scale, how big is "different" for you? What are the boundaries, the borders, the proprieties, and customs, the edges in your mind that define different for you? What are

Hmmmmm… Whom could I become?

86

things that very few people know about you—the things about you that aren't same or similar, the things that make you different?

How different would others see you in the face of these insights?

"The similarities between me and my father are different."
Dale Berra, Yogi Berra's son

This is one of the key aspects of the Me, Inc.® process: seeing and valuing yourself as someone unique and special and different. Identifying your unique beliefs and principles. Discovering the unique set of strengths and skills that makes you really you. Appreciating more fully who you are. Creating a vision and mission for yourself that only you have, that no one else is thinking about, and that no one else is doing.

By first seeing different in ourselves, we learn to value different, and from there we can learn to see and value different in others, in the thinking of others, and finally, in the ideas and changes that others come up with that may strike us as very, very different—as 3-Sigma mindshifts for us.

A good exercise to transition your thinking from Level 5 (copying) to Level 6 (different) is to focus on yourself as someone who is in fact different.

Be different.

Become different.

How are you different? Make a list...

Levels of Change

1-Sigma   Continuous Improvement

    Level 1

    Level 2

    Level 3

2-Sigma   Process Reengineering

    Level 4

    Level 5

3-Sigma   Breakout and Breakthrough

    Level 6

    Level 7

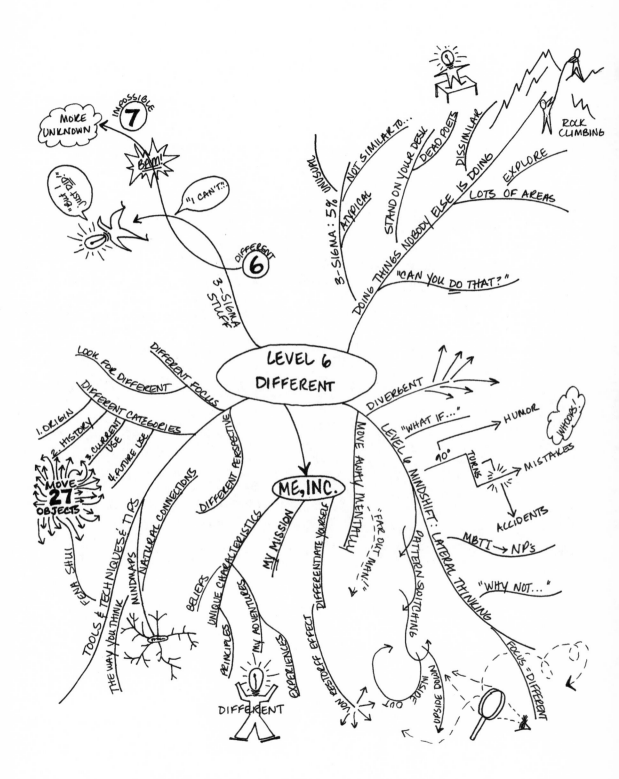

LEVEL 6: DIFFERENT

UNDERSTANDING LEVEL 6

You're effective and efficient. You've improved and cut out waste. You've copied the best and adapted it to fit. Now, what's the next step to change, to really be innovative, to break the mold? You have to come up with something different, a totally new idea that isn't like anything you know of. Really different—unlike in form, quality, amount, or nature to anything else. Dissimilar. Distinct. Separate. Unusual. You can't find ideas like this because they don't exist—you have to come up with them yourself.

> *"When you come to a fork in the road, take it."*
>
> **Yogi Berra**

Generally speaking, Level 6 changes also involve significant commitments of time, effort, and resources. They're not typically changes that can be made immediately. Statistically, there are not many of them—they're the start of 3-Sigma. They're rare and special. And they're radical.

The majority of change and change ideas (some 68 percent—1-Sigma) come from the lower levels—primarily Levels 1, 2, and 3. These are smaller, more incremental changes that don't fundamentally affect the entire organization. Level 4 and 5 changes typically make a bigger impact. Level 6 changes transform. Level 1, 2, and 3 changes keep a company moving along the road of continuous improvement. But when an organization is stuck, no longer making money or losing market share, it's time for something different—Level 6.

Level 6 thinkers and doers are easy to recognize. They're habitual rule breakers. They have a lot of ideas, but many of the ideas are so far out there (out in the 3-Sigma area) that it causes most people (Level 1, 2, and 3 thinkers in their 1-Sigma world) to view them as nuts. They aren't nuts; they just tend to blurt out their ideas before they are fully formed. A lot of things don't really make sense for them until they say them out loud.

It's psychological vomit. But, if you're willing to poke around in it, you might find a diamond. At the other end of the scale, Level 1, 2, and 3 thinkers stifle their ideas because they edit and re-edit them before they are willing to let other people hear what they have to say. Unlike the lower level thinkers, Level 6 people don't

90

really care what you think about their idea—it's just important for them to share it. They're "B+" thinkers.

Level 6 people tend to have a lot of different hobbies and interests. They'll be aficionados of something. They may be musical. If so, they probably play a couple of different instruments, not particularly well but well enough that they enjoy it. Their offices will reflect their interests. They'll tend to like different, more abstract artwork. Their desks, shelves, and filing cabinets will be covered with piles (not stacks) of information.

They probably never look inside their filing cabinets. With them, out of sight is out of mind.

They don't want the furniture that everyone else has in their office. It's not that they want something more prestigious, just something different. They might bring in something from home like an old rocking chair. When you come into their office, you'll often have to clean something off to find a place to sit down.

Level 6 doers and thinkers are constantly sharing their ideas. "Have you seen this?" "Did you hear that?" You won't find them sitting down and reading a book from cover to cover like a Level 1, 2, or 3 thinker. Instead, they'll have several books going at once and will skip around reading a few pages, or sometimes chapters from each, not necessarily in any particular order.

If you have a casual day at the office, the Level 6 folks will get really casual and very different—and not just wild T-shirts and socks. Even on a noncasual day, their ties will give them away. Think playful. Mickey Mouse watches were once a strong indicator of Level 6 and Level 7 thinkers, but they don't seem to be quite as prevalent as they were several years ago. If there's a new trend in dress or sports equipment or tennis shoes, they'll be on to it.

Even when I was in the air force, my Level 6 traits managed to leak out. The air force would periodically test uniforms with a defined test group somewhere in the world. Wherever it was, I would manage to get it. I loved being

Tip! Watch for "messy"

Efficient

What can you start doing right now to become more efficient?

...BLUE SLIP

different. When I worked with NATO, the Brits had a great sweater called a "woolie-pully," and I managed to get hold of one. I got away with wearing it by simply telling people it was a test item. (And it was—I was testing it.)

In a group, Level 6 thinkers and doers are stretchers. They'll pull the lower level thinkers past their normal realm of thinking. When your company is trying to move to higher levels of change, you have to have the stretchers in there. They'll push the numbers of ideas way up—the volume—and people at lower levels will be able to piggyback onto their ideas and refine them. And if the organization can control itself and suspend judgment (PIN), you'll often find a diamond.

LEVEL 6 TOOL #1: DIFF*F*ERENT FOCUS

If you want to achieve breakout thinking, focus on what's different about previous experiences or solutions, not what's similar.

LEVEL 6 TOOL #2: DIFF*F*ERENT PERSPECTIVE

In the movie *The Dead Poets Society*, Robin Williams (as John Keating, the poetry teacher) stretched his students' thinking by standing on top of his desk. "Why do I stand up here? I stand upon my desk to constantly remind myself that we must look at the world in a different way," Keating said. "You see, the world looks very different from here. You don't believe me? Come see for yourselves." And the whole class climbs up on the desk and begins to see things in a different way. On Thinking Expeditions, this is a tool that has produced great results. We have everyone stand on the tabletops and on their chairs to get them to physically, deliberately look at things in a different way. It's dramatic and energizing. Once you've done something different, the next time you do it won't be difficult anymore. For adults in business, it's crazy. People laugh and have fun with it and break out of their normal thought patterns immediately. And they get the beginnings of breakout ideas.

92

In our School for Innovators, we've pushed this type of lateral thinking of standing on the desk to the very edge of Level 6. Working with Mike Donahue, owner and director of the Colorado Mountain School in Estes Park, we've integrated three half days of rock climbing into the curriculum. Getting people to climb a sheer rock face or clamber by rope up to the summit of a mountain actually borders on Level 7 for most people. It's so different that it's something they can't imagine themselves ever doing. It gives them a totally different perspective—not only of the world, but of themselves and how they perceive risk.

> *"A great thought begins by seeing something differently, with a shift of the mind's eye."*
> Albert Einstein

LEVEL 6 TOOL #3: CATEGORICALLY DIFFERENT

We all tend to notice things in terms of categories that we have personally developed and have become comfortable with over time. These categories then function as lenses in terms of what we see and how we see. To raise your awareness of different, to notice more different things, or to notice them differently, create new categories, and begin looking at objects "through" them. Win Wenger, in his book *The Einstein Factor*, suggests four such categories: origin, history, current use, and future use. When we see something, normal thinking sees it in its current use. "Origin" moves backward in time and raises the question of how the object was made or where it came from. "History" might look at how long it has been this way or who has used it or how it was used. "Future use" moves your thinking into new possibilities and opportunities.

Level 6 ideas are like those Transformer action figures—they keep building and changing. In 1990, a Level 6 Exxon service station owner came up with an idea to sell Supreme, the new high octane fuel. It was a simple slogan: "Think Red." Prior to then, Exxon stations had two-hose pumps. One was blue, the other was black. The blue had always been high test. To handle the new supreme, they

---

Competency

Thinking simultaneously at Level 1 and Level 2

Level 1 - Effectiveness: Doing the right things
Level 2 - Efficiency: Doing things right

installed new pumps with three handles and the third one, the highest octane, was red.

The station owner created a sticker for the pump: "Think Red." And buttons for his cashiers: "Think Red." His customers started asking questions and soon learned about supreme—the 98 octane designed for high-performance vehicles such as BMWs and Porsches. Supreme sales at his station jumped better than 30 percent in a very short period of time. Exxon eventually bought the rights from the owner and took the idea to Houston where it was tested with a full-blown campaign: red hats, T-shirts, and more. Exxon hooked up with Big Red soda and with a local radio station, KRED. The idea was tremendously successful. Big Red sold more soda during the test quarter than they'd sold the previous year. KRED's listeners, young and "high octaned" themselves, fed a new market of young Exxon credit card holders who obviously liked different and a high octane image—and Exxon never would have thought about tapping them.

LEVEL 6 TOOL #4: FENG SHUI

Feng Shui is the oriental art of placement. If you are stuck in a rut or an unpleasant situation, if you can't change or get to different, move twenty-seven objects in your home that have not been moved in the last year. It will enhance your ability to move forward in life, to change. By making twenty-seven small, seemingly nonsignificant changes in your life, which afterward you notice on a daily basis, you will constantly raise your own awareness of the need for change and that things are easily made different.

Sometimes you have to climb to a Level 6 change by moving through lower levels of change first. Several years ago I ran a Thinking Expedition for several very big oil companies that had formed a team to look at ways to reduce the costs of producing and exporting an energy product in the Arctic. One of the three joint project managers had contacted us and asked us to design an out-of-the-box thinking workshop that would make the joint team comfortable with divergent thinking processes and 3-Sigma ideas. We created

Move 27 things in your house to remind yourself to change...

a Thinking Expedition built around the 7 Levels of Change—a metaphorical push into the unknown of Arctic field operations in which all normal operating rules would be thrown out.

The Thinking Expedition was split into two three-day operations, two months apart. Stage I was used to form up the team, shift their thinking, train them in innovation tools and techniques, and then push forward into the unknown by slowly diverging and exploring up through the 7 Levels of Change. Major breakthroughs began occurring as early as at Level 4—stopping doing normal things and cutting out processes and procedures that had been the industry standard for years. The potential for very large cost savings, which this level of thinking uncovered, surprisingly pushed the team's thinking first lower into Level 3 and the exploration of general technological improvements in a wide range of areas, looking at stuff that now would function under Arctic conditions but which previously would not have. We looked backward down technological shift paths into some black holes of traditional engineering thinking.

From those discoveries, and there were many, thinking rapidly shifted back into considering wide ranges of new technologies and work processes that were not being used (Level 6) in the Arctic by oil companies at all—but which other kinds of companies were using under severe conditions. The Level 3 and Level 6 technologies and processes were then forced into impossible combinations to solve impossible problems in ways that wouldn't work or couldn't be done (Level 7).

LEVEL 6 TOOL #5: DIVERGENT CONVERGENCE

The Thinking Expedition was resumed two months later with Stage II after the team had some time to work through all the ideas, research the more unusual areas, and flesh many of them out into an operating concept or technical approach. Stage II took on a very different "nonfocus" compared with a normal project of this nature: divergent convergence. Instead of focusing on developing the "good" ideas

Stage I Divergent (normal)

Continuous improvement is about CHANGE!

95

that had come out of Stage I—the ideas that clearly would work or that management would buy—the team went for the fringes. The idea was to focus on developing strategies and action plans only on the 3-Sigma, highly divergent ideas—the Level 6 and Level 7 concepts and changes.

The breakout results were conservatively estimated to be changes of 30 to 40 percent in operating costs with long-term potential savings in excess of $5 billion.

One of the breakthrough tools we used throughout the Arctic Thinking Expedition was Mindmapping. Mindmaps worked so well for the team that at the end we summarized everything we'd done—all the BIG ideas and results—with one huge Mindmap that covered a whole wall. That has since led to our use of Mindmapping as a mainstay tool in all succeeding Thinking Expeditions.

A Mindmap is a visual representation of your thoughts about a particular topic arranged in such a way that you can see all of them on a single page. Mindmaps use no sentences. Instead, they rely on icons, key words, and a spiderweb-like connecting framework to tie everything together. They spread out like a spiderweb. Mindmaps actually have tremendous structure even though they may not appear that way. They are a visual flow of consciousness, never really finished because your thinking is never finished.

Why do they work? They develop the way you think. You have an idea—it sparks something new. Your train of thought jumps around creating new branches on the Mindmap. Mindmapping is real different. The concept originated with Tony Buzan, who developed the technique based on research that showed the brain fundamentally works with key concepts or "chunks" of information and ideas in an interrelated and integrated way. Your brain doesn't come up with ideas in a linear fashion—it jumps around. Mindmapping accommodates that and allows you to use your whole brain—both your creative and analytical sides—by freeing you from the constraints of linear thinking.

Stage II Different! The trick was to also evaluate differently and implement differently

Take a quick look at the mindmaps at the end of each chapter

96

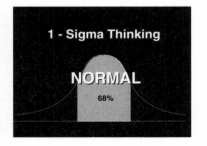

① Key word in all CAPS

② Connecting ideas only first letter is CAPitalized

③ Next level of idea use all lower case letters

④ Use icons, little pictures

⑤ Use color

1 - Sigma Thinking

NORMAL

68%

LEVEL 6 TOOL #6: MINDMAPS

How do you create a Mindmap? Start with a blank sheet of paper. Set the focus either by drawing a small icon capturing the essence of your focus in the middle of the page or writing down the topic or subject you want to focus on, and circle it.

Begin brainstorming with yourself by thinking of major aspects of the topic. Draw a leg outward from the center and write the main thrust of one of the major aspects along the leg. Print the key word describing it in all capital letters. Continue brainstorming and bring some connecting points off the main leg as smaller legs or points that connect with (expanding or refining) the main leg. Capitalize the first letter of these words or phrases (this brings surprising structure to the Mindmap). If further expansions or refinements occur to you that are related to these, bring a third-order leg off them and print the words or phrases on this leg in lowercase letters. Headline your ideas. Limit them to one or two key words as much as possible. Keep adding simple icons, stick figures, little picturettes wherever you can. Pictures significantly reinforce your ability to remember the Mindmap and help others understand it quickly.

As you are doing this, you are likely to think of other major thrusts. When you do, immediately add them as more main legs and begin connecting ideas and thoughts to them. Use a different color for each new major leg and all its branches and sub-branches. This makes the Mindmap even more visual. Keep using icons and symbols to emphasize points as much as possible—simple little stick figures and primitive drawings.

You can either brainstorm all the major lines first and then the branches on each (the more linear approach), or brainstorm a main leg and its branches and sub-branches, or jump around randomly from one line to another as the ideas you're generating cause other ideas to pop off. When you have completed the Mindmap, you can add more structure to it by circling each main leg and all its sub-branches and using different colors to set off each grouping. For example, take a look at the Mindmaps that introduce each level of change throughout this book. Now, make your own!

Tip!

Watch out! Mindmaps can be stressful for more traditionally structured people (strong KAI adaptive scores and ISTJ/ESTJ engineers—see Getting Ready for Change, page 129), but they are a nonthreatening way to stretch them to a higher level of change. On Thinking Expeditions we pair people by opposite KAI or MBTI scores and have them explain their Mindmaps to each other. We've discovered that once they've worked through a Mindmap by pairing up with someone of the opposite style or type, the stress seems to drop off, and we frequently see real breakout thinking occur. And a Mindmap can readily be transformed into a linear, sequential, very normally structured, engineering-like outline (a reassuring thought for the more convergent).

Technique:

To transform from Mindmap to outline, use a colored marker to broadly enclose each major leg and all its sub-branches as a main topic. Then number each major area and, within each area, number its sub-branches and all their ideas to reflect their order and relationships. At that Point, by following the numbered sequences, you can word-process it into a normally structured outline.

Mindmapping is a great tool for understanding a problem and is especially powerful in exploring the issues, challenges, obstacles, goals, and objectives imbedded in a problem, especially when the interrelationships are unclear. Seventy-five to 85 percent of learning is visual, so when we need to communicate big, complex ideas, a visual tool like a Mindmap is very powerful. We teach it to guides in the School for Innovators as the best tool for interacting with Thinking Expedition clients and sponsors for helping them clarify the scope of their exploration and discovery area.

Interestingly, Mindmaps are such strong visual and imprinting tools that very often a whole map can be recalled

NOTE- High recall, remembering with mind mapping

98

Tip! What to do with only 15 minutes...

or reconstructed without looking at it again. Because of this, Mindmaps are a powerful tool for interactions to help explain out-of-the-box ideas. The following story is an illustration of just how powerful Mindmaps can be.

Anna Natsis, a senior civilian manager in the Defense Information Systems Agency (DISA), used a Mindmap a few weeks after graduating from the School for Innovators in August of 1994, to brief the agency's new director, a three-star air force general, on her functions then as chief of Quality Customer Service. She described Lieutenant General Al Edmonds as a dynamo who had little time for all the managers to tell their stories. She was given only fifteen minutes.

"I knew I had to make my story stick and wanted to do it DIFFERENTLY than everyone else," Anna says. "They had all trooped in with the inevitable military-like charts and view graphs, listing numbers, functions, challenges, etc."

Anna decided to use a Mindmap to cover "a lot in one look versus a lot of talk."

"I chose to use a small posterlike chart, approximately twenty inches by twenty-six inches. It was white on one side and gold on the back. I laid out the main branches: People, Issues, Customers, Initiatives, Opportunities, Challenges, and Functions. With the help of my folks (who somewhat questioned my risk taking), we laid out all the facets of these key branches, using different colors, of course. It turned out to be a great brainstorming session for us as we in essence developed our vision for the organization," Anna says.

Since General Edmonds was unknown to Anna, she was taking a big risk. However, she knew he had a reputation for being visionary and an out-of-the-box thinker.

"I rolled the chart up into a scroll, gold side showing, and wrapped a blue cloth ribbon around it (air force colors: blue and gold!). When I arrived for my appointment, there is no question that the secretary and executive assistant to the director thought something was wrong. I had no view graphs and would need no view graph machine. Surely Ms. Natsis had lost it.

LEVEL 3
Improving

Doing Things Better

"When I entered the director's office, I'm sure he was wondering a bit, too. I spoke a minute or two describing what a Mindmap attempts to do and then rolled it out for him. Needless to say, he was a bit surprised! As I ran around the topics, focusing only on a few, I knew he'd connected when he said, 'Wow!'"

Some background: Anna's director had come to her agency to leapfrog the telecommunications and information systems organization into the twenty-first century on his watch. Part of his mission was to bring information to deployed war fighters rapidly, reliably, securely, and in an understandable manner. As such, General Edmonds was championing a program designed to provide the war fighter a "fused picture of his battle space," thus eliminating the need for many computers and pounds and pounds of data.

"When I finished with my fifteen minutes, what General Edmonds said made my day," Anna says. "He said that what I had presented was not a Mindmap but a 'Fused Picture of the Quality Customer Service Battlespace.'"

Recently, Anna was promoted to her current senior executive service (SES) rank, the civilian equivalent of a one-star general. She believes that the promotion has a direct connection back to how she explained her concepts to her new director using a Mindmap.

ROLF'S THEORY OF RELATIVITY

Anna's story about General Edmonds illustrates how relative Level 6 thinking can be. Though a Mindmap was different to her director, he immediately transferred the concept to his own definition and made it familiar. Something is only different if you don't know about it. Someone else may have known about it for years. To them it might be Level 2 efficiency—doing the right things right.

I find it interesting that senior people will often say that what they are doing is different because no one in their industry is doing it. But they aren't aware of what is going on in other industries. When introducing Level 6 thinking, techniques, changes, keep in mind how relative different can be for people.

Different is relative

100

As pointed out with the Arctic Thinking Expedition story, Mindmapping can be used with groups to review and refocus a topic or subject that the group has been working on for some time. Similarly, Mindmaps are great summary tools in classroom situations (see pages 153-156, the case study on Gwen Keith's junior high school in Houston, Texas).

Technique:

With groups, an approach that works well is to construct a large Mindmap out of six sheets of flip-chart paper taped together on a wall. Start by having two key members of the group, working as a pair, write down ideas the rest of the group calls out in the form of key words. The two group members get the initial form of the Mindmap going. Then they can engage everyone in writing and drawing on the Mindmap, calling out the key words and phrases as they develop legs and sublegs.

Very recently, working with my church's long-range vision group, we hit on the concept of using a very large Mindmap (5 ft x 12 ft) to engage and involve everyone in the congregation in visioning the future. We had already identified eight major strategic interest areas, using Blue Slips and a Five-Minute Meeting, and then planned to draw those as "starter" legs for a skeleton Mindmap to spark everyone's thinking. We laid the Mindmap out on three sheets of foam core board so it would be sturdy and portable, made smaller versions of it (8 1/2 x 11) to insert in the weekly bulletins, and planned to launch it at the annual church picnic. We would then continue using it for the entire month to give people time to reflect and engage in time at their own comfort level and style.

On picnic Sunday, Rick Hartmann, our pastor, opened his sermon by holding up the bulletin-sized Mindmap and talking about it. He set the stage for everyone to add to the big Mindmap during the picnic, and—it worked! By the end of the picnic, markers were flying, and a good-sized crowd was gathered around the Mindmap.

The next Sunday, Tim Anderson, our out-of-the-box assistant pastor and a graduate of our most recent School for

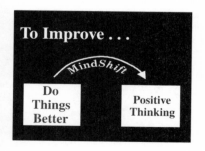

Innovators (Expedition XVIII, August 1996), had the big Mindmap moved right up to the front of the church and tied his entire sermon into it. A few weeks before, after returning from the school in Estes Park, Colorado, he had already set the stage for different by giving a mindshifting sermon wearing his Thinking Expedition vest and ⌐HIИK hat. In the meantime, Doreen Leptien, our deaconess, had engaged two of the committees (Education and Children & Youth) during their regular meetings in developing their own Mindmaps of what their ministry really was, what they were currently doing, and what they hoped to do. She made them work from a completely blank slate, and only when their Mindmaps were finished did she let them move over into budget realities. The two committees teamed up and began very naturally working together for the first time.

That was followed the next week by a church council off-site, which I guided (using their KAI scores), and which built further on the big Mindmap. The council members and all committee members then began adding to the visioning Mindmap each week. Because the pastors, Rick and Tim, continued tying the Mindmap into their sermons, the whole congregation became more and more actively engaged. Eventually, we used nominal voting techniques to engage everyone in focusing and prioritizing the pathways we would follow into the future. BIG Ideas were developed with supporting action plans, and we have some pretty exciting changes ranging from Level 1 to Level 7 now under way at Holy Cross Lutheran Church in Houston.

In the end, it wasn't just the Mindmap that was a Level 6 change. From the congregation's point of view (Rolf's Theory of Relativity), everything we tried was different for most people.

LEVEL 6 TOOL #7: BUILD THE MOUNTAIN, THEN CLIMB IT

Sometimes you have to clearly define your challenge—build your mountain—before you can begin to climb. Often when you generate all the interrelated issues, challenges, obstacles, opportunities, ideas, and history associated with

written on blue slips

the mess that is your challenge—the mountain—the solution becomes as clear as a trail to the top. The following story shows the way.

Steve Weichert at the Exxon Benicia Refinery in the Bay Area and a 1989 graduate of one of our very early School for Innovators sessions, called us in 1995 with the idea of running a Thinking Expedition focused on the turnaround maintenance cycle. Benicia is essentially a single-thread operation; when major periodic maintenance is scheduled, the entire refinery must shut down, and production stops. Huge numbers of contractors descend on the facility in barely controlled chaos. Steve's objectives for the Thinking Expedition were to significantly reduce the time required (Level 2 and Level 4 changes) for the maintenance operation or to find a way to perform the critical maintenance functions without completely stopping production (Level 6).

Two key elements of every Thinking Expedition are "building the mountain range" out of Blue Slips and then "route finding" up the right mountain. We divide the group up into subteams of four to six people (by similar KAI scores), and then have the subteams do this by generating all the interrelated issues, challenges, obstacles, opportunities, ideas, and history associated with the mess that is the exploration area of the Thinking Expedition, or the focus. Then they integrate and synthesize them on tabletops into a coherent whole—the mountain range. It was during this part of the Thinking Expedition that the major mindshifts and breakout thinking occurred in the team of engineers. Real clarity around the complexity of the problem leaped out as the route finding through the mountain range uncovered the chain of events that would have to happen before any compressed turnaround objectives could really be achieved—the ah ha! effect was profound (Level 6 thinking). The results of the Thinking Expedition were much more in the engineering mindshifts and resolution of the problem definition and understanding than in actual solutions and action plans.

Building mountain ranges is a very messy, very visual, but also very kinesthetic (the "building" part) exercise.

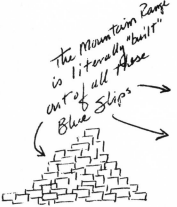

the Mountain Range is literally "built" out of all these Blue Slips →

THINKING ABOUT THINKING

Level 6 thinking is different thinking—thinking that is unlike in style, type, form, process, quality, amount, or nature to anything else. It's thinking that reverses basic assumptions and accepted logic or reasoning. It's thinking that is distinct or separate, particularly in style and process. It's unusual thinking.

Level 6 thinking is intentional.

In the middle of writing this, WHAM! the new issue of *Fortune* magazine arrived. The September 30, 1996, issue. The only business magazine I read religiously. But, it's clearly not *Fortune*. It's different. What happened?

"The issue of *Fortune* you hold in your hand is indeed quite different from any you have seen before—in typography, color, palette, organization, even size," *Fortune* told its readers.

Wow! I'm writing about different, about Level 6 change. I'm already late on the deadline to the publisher and BAM! I can't believe this is happening. There are no accidents. This is uncanny!

"For the past eighteen months we have been striving to do nothing less than reinvent the modern business magazine—to become the best business magazine in the world that happens to be about business," *Fortune*'s editor goes on to say.

Do you remember how you felt when you picked up the mail that day and there was *Fortune*? CHANGE! How did you deal with it? What did you do? Where did you flip first in the magazine? Did you try to find an old, comfortable section to read first—the one you always used to read? Or did you go right for what was really different, stuff you didn't recognize at all but that looked interesting? Reflect for a moment. Can you remember any of your reactions? How did you handle change at Level 6?

I read the "Editor's Desk" first. What are they doing? Where's their thinking? What are the changes behind the changes?

If you're like me, you've been reading *Fortune* for a long time. Good stuff. Smooth reading. Learningful. Good quotes. On top of things. Articles to tear out and save or copy and

104

send to people. Better hang on to this issue. Put it back out on your desk as a visual reminder of Level 6 thinking and change in your life.

Level 6 thinking is also lateral thinking. It's pattern switching within a patterning system. It's thinking which approaches a problem or concept from a different perspective or point of view, including backward. It's thinking which deliberately moves across accepted channels of thought or cuts across patterns instead of moving up or down with them.

MINDSHIFT

The mindshift required at Level 6 is a shift to lateral thinking—moving away from, disconnecting, moving off to the side and thinking about something from a completely different angle. Looking at things out of the corner of your eye. Standing on your mental desk. Upside down. Inside out. Constantly looking at the world from different angles in different ways.

Consider the following diagram. To get different results, you have to do things different. To do things no one else is doing, you first have to think different. To do things different requires lateral thinking.

At Level 6, you shift into 3-Sigma. You are choosing to do, to think different. You are moving beyond average, beyond normal, beyond interesting, and into different. You are turning away from rules, regulations, conventional wisdom, and structure. You are becoming proactive with your thinking, transforming your ideas and creativity into action in non-normal, discontinuous, unorthodox, and unusual ways.

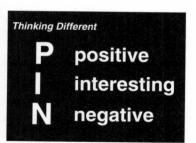

LEVEL 6 PROS & CONS

Level 6 is exciting. It's where breakouts have their roots. When you begin working at this level, you are moving into the unknown of big possibilities, unexpected opportunities, major transitions, surprises, and areas where all bets are off. Here are the WOWs! with huge impact—in dollars, time savings, new markets, and totally new directions. In fact, because Level 6 is about different, you really have no idea what will happen or what you'll get.

Cons? The drawbacks to Level 6 are myriad. For one, it's generally much more difficult to sell ideas at this level just because they are so unfamiliar and strange to normal thinking. Ideas at this level are different from 95 percent of all other ideas. There's nothing to compare them to—they're untested. People have nothing to compare them to give them the certainty that they will work. The likelihood of failure appears much higher here.

Because they tend to generate a lot of ideas, Level 6 thinkers often roll right over other people's ideas and can easily dominate a team. To many, they seem to be wasting time because so many of their ideas will "clearly" never be used. Level 6 thinkers know that, but it doesn't bother them. Further, without realizing it, they can cause a great deal of stress by putting much more stretch on lower level thinkers than they can handle. Differences in KAI scores become very apparent at Level 6.

Level 6 changes can be expensive, often tied to new technology. Remember, most Level 6 ideas come from people who are idea generators, not implementers. And sometimes Level 6 thinkers get so enamored with doing something different that they do it just for the sake of doing it.

ME, INC.®

Your challenge here is to differentiate yourself. What are the truly unique factors and experiences, beliefs, principles, goals, and strengths that make you YOU? What's your mission? Most of the time, you'll find that your mission is

Level 6 Ideas... Nothing to compare them with

106

unique. It applies to you and your unique vision, situation, business, and differentness. Your values, principles, strengths, and beliefs all add up to support you in carrying out your mission. Go back and finalize your mission now. Keep it to one short sentence. Whittle it down to its essence. Practice saying it out loud.

> *"The more you're like yourself, the less you're like somebody else."*
>
> Anonymous

TRANSITION TO LEVEL 7: DIFFERENT—IMPOSSIBLE

When a change or idea is not only different but also is so different that there is no known way to do it, when major obstacles leap out as soon as you start looking at the realities of implementation, when much of what you're looking at simply can't be done, you've shifted into the realm of impossible, the arena of magic and miracles.

Moving from Level 6 to Level 7 is a transition from the possible but incomparable to the improbable and unpredictable. Where Level 6 may have been uncomfortable, Level 7 is downright scary and full of ninety-degree turns—real BAM! stuff that blows you away when it happens because it can't.

You know you've reached Level 7 when you can't—but you do.

THINKING ABOUT THINKING

Improved Thinking

· **Ask for ideas**
  - **Ask for suggestions**
  - **Actually listen to other people**

- LEVEL 3 THINKING

Levels of Change

LEVEL 7: Breakthrough-Doing things that can't be done
LEVEL 6: Different-Doing things that haven't been done before
LEVEL 5: Adapting-Doing things other people are doing
LEVEL 4: Cutting-Doing away with things
LEVEL 3: Improving-Doing things better
LEVEL 2: Efficiency-Doing things right
LEVEL 1: Effectiveness-Doing the right things

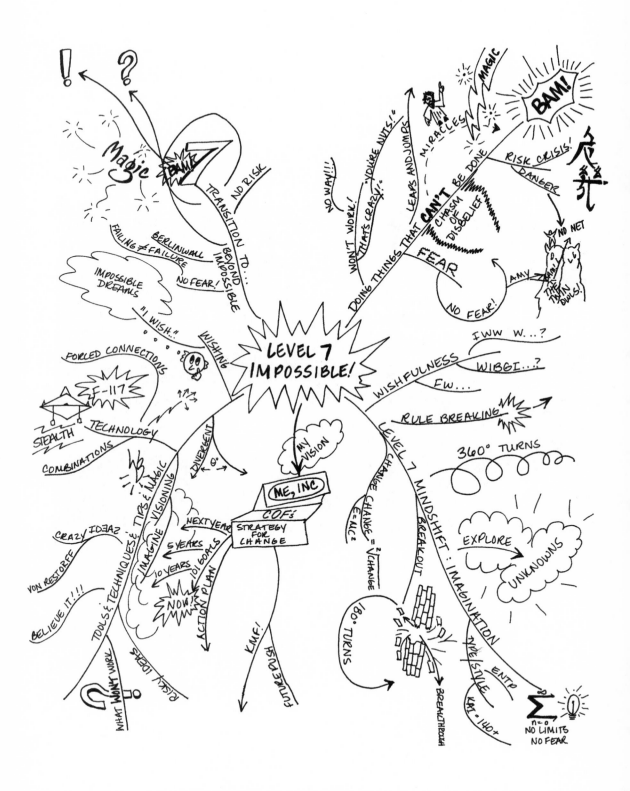

LEVEL 7: IMPOSSIBLE

DOING THINGS THAT CAN'T BE DONE

UNDERSTANDING LEVEL 7

In August 1992, while rock climbing with my family on the Twin Owls in Estes Park, Colorado, we learned what Level 7 really meant. Some six hundred feet up a shear rock face, my eight–year-old daughter, Amy, froze. We'd reached the end of a long ledge that tapered down to about two inches wide and sort of disappeared into a crack around the corner. The rock face dropped off fast from the ledge into the valley farther and farther below. The wind was blowing, our clothes and jackets flapping. Cars and people in the parking lot we had started from looked smaller than ants.

Amy was tied into the rope out in front of me, and Mike Donahue, our guide, was another one hundred feet ahead and up, out of sight. Amy looked down, realized where she was, and saw only that it was impossible for her to move—pure Level 7. I tried everything I could think of to coach and coax her on, but she wouldn't budge. She was absolutely paralyzed, and she kept looking down at the ground six hundred feet below.

I finally gave up. Actually, I had a mindshift. Logic and reason weren't working and trying to restore her

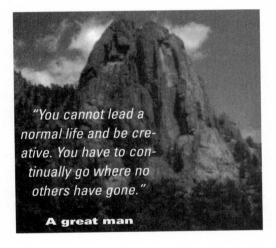

"You cannot lead a normal life and be creative. You have to continually go where no others have gone."

A great man

110

Impossible? Tip — Do what can't be done

confidence wasn't working, so I tried to move into some parallel thinking with Amy at Level 7. What couldn't I do? I certainly couldn't just abandon her, leave here there clinging to bare rocks, so I did. I said, "Amy, my foot's slipping. I can't stay here with you any longer. If you can't go up, I'm going to have to leave you here and go back down the ledge." And I took a step backward.

BAM! Amy came to instant life, made a move—BAM!—made the next move and—ZIP!—shot around the corner and up the crack like a squirrel (Level 7). She was all grins, moving on and full of adrenaline as Mike coached her on up. The rest was easy. We were there. She'd done the impossible. Her summit had been down below, not up at the top. Wow! You never get a second chance at a first experience.

There is risk to Level 7. Sometimes when there is no way to get out of a situation, it takes a leap of faith. Jump and the net will appear. We use rock climbing as an integral part of the School for Innovators, both literally and as a metaphor to help people think the impossible. When they do the impossible, when they reach the summit, then nothing is hard anymore.

Aside from fear, some other big catalysts for Level 7 change are humor, accidents, and mistakes. When you are intending to do A, and B happens instead, when you are traveling down one path and an accident turns you ninety degrees, when a punch line really hits you—there are opportunities for Level 7 ideas to break through.

Think about some things that can't be done. We can't finish this project by Monday—we can't speed up the delivery date—we can't change the process—it won't work here. Then think about what would have to change to be able to accomplish those things. That's how you move toward the impossible.

Nick Sealey, New Zealand market manager for KFC/Pizza Hut and a School for Innovators graduate (January 1993), says that the tools his company has taken away from the School for Innovators have changed the way they treat ideas and things that can't be done or won't

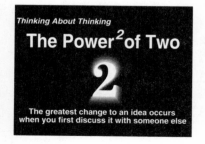

Thinking About Thinking

The Power²of Two

2

The greatest change to an idea occurs when you first discuss it with someone else work. "We're not afraid to try things or to really empower people," Nick says.

In 1994, Nick oversaw the introduction of home delivery into Kentucky Fried Chicken in New Zealand. He'd been told that it just didn't work for KFC worldwide.

Nick had taken time out and had done some retrospective thinking. In New Zealand ten to fifteen years ago, 60 percent of KFC business was in meal replacement for families of four who would come out to eat or pick up buckets for carryout. That slipped down to 25 percent when TV dinners and other ready-made meals made inroads. Looking at some other trends and noticing shifts in consumer habits in their stores, Nick felt his part of the world was different and had different potential, so he pushed to at least get the home delivery concept tested in Australia. The Australians then passed their learnings and experiences over to the Kiwis. KFC New Zealand took that template, adapted, modified, and built on it (Level 5 copying). They ran several Creative Problem Solving sessions with both staff and management, focused on roadblocks to success, and began implementing the BIG ideas they came up with.

They stopped treating home delivery as an attachment to the store business, made it a separate and distinct business (Level 4 change—stopping doing things and Level 6 change—a different business), and homed in on people, equipment, and some low-level technology ideas. All these changes combined to be a real Level 7 change, something that wouldn't work and couldn't be done. By 1996 KFC Home Delivery Units in New Zealand were pushing four times the sales in the United States.

"The key is people, their ideas, and not constraining yourself by being judgmental no matter how outlandish those ideas may seem at the time," Nick says.

LEVEL 7 TOOL #1: MAKE A WISH

Wishing is a powerful way to expand your ability to think and do the impossible at Level 7. I mentioned this back at

112

Level 6 in the context of Mess-Finding. Now we'll look at wishes as a Level 7 tool to achieve breakthrough thinking. Don't be afraid to make a wish and see where it takes you. This is how some incredible products started. "I wish we had an airplane that they couldn't see and couldn't shoot down. An invisible airplane, yeah, that's what I wish we had." What would we need to have that wish come true? A new material that doesn't reflect radar. A different wing angle that doesn't reflect radar. BAM! Suddenly the impossible is possible. When you solve those challenges, you have the Stealth fighter—Lockheed Skunkworks' F-117.

In Iraq, the Stealth fighter flew more than two thousand combat missions and came away without a scratch. Able to go in and out without being seen or shot at, the pilots could take much more time and be much more precise (Level 1 and 2 doing), and achieve significantly improved accuracy (Level 3 doing) to produce Level 7 results. With less than 3 percent of the total aircraft in the theater of operations, they hit more than 40 percent of the strategic pinpoint targets with amazing accuracy. 3-Sigma leverage.

What would be the equivalent of a Stealth fighter in your operations? What could it do to your bottom-line results?

LEVEL 7 TOOL #2: THE CRAZY IDEA

After making wishes, getting crazy can be the next best way to solve an impossible challenge. Start with a "mess"—your impossible challenge.

Step 1: Messing around

Write your mess as a short statement on a Blue Slip and label it "Mess." Now, mess around with your mess. Restate it at least three different ways. Look at it from three different angles and try to get more different with each one. Write each problem restatement on a Blue Slip.

Step 2: Thinking outside the box

Look at your four different Blue Slips stating your problem and think, "Given this mess, what's the craziest idea I can come up with?" This idea should be so crazy that if you told

Tip! Mess around more with your problems

it to someone, they would think you're nuts. Now, write your Crazy Idea down on a Blue Slip and label it CRAZY.

Not all ideas are good ideas. But not all bad ideas are totally useless. Take a hard look at your Crazy Idea. On a scale of zero to one hundred, with zero being totally useless and one hundred being perfect, where does your Crazy Idea sit? Grade yourself and write the score on your Crazy Idea Blue Slip. If it's anything but zero, there's some small piece of value in it.

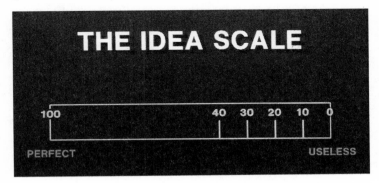

Step 3: The question of novelty

Crazy is different. So is creativity. Creativity can be defined as coming up with ideas that are novel and useful—novel in that they are significantly different from the normal kinds of ideas that you have. How novel is your Crazy Idea?

Take another Blue Slip and label it NOVEL and write down the main element of novelty in your Crazy Idea. What makes it significantly different—novel—from other ideas you've had. What makes it crazy?

Step 4: Forcing perspective

Now take another Blue Slip and label it USEFUL and write down one thing that is useful about your Crazy Idea. What was it about the idea that kept you from giving it a score of zero? If you did give your idea a zero, make yourself stretch. Lie about its usefulness if necessary. Make something up.

Take another look at your idea. It really is pretty weak, isn't it? What's one thing that's missing from your idea that

114

if it were included would significantly move it toward the perfect end of the scale? Write that on a third Blue Slip labeled MISSING.

Put a paper clip on your USEFUL and MISSING Blue Slips so they don't accidentally get mixed in with anyone else's.

Step 5: The sanity check

At this point you may find a "sanity check" useful. Just how crazy is your idea, really? Turn the CRAZY Blue Slip face-down and exchange it with the person sitting next to you for their Crazy Idea. Turn your partner's Blue Slip over and read it. Don't discuss it, just read it.

Step 6: The von Restorff effect

Research by a German psychologist, H. von Restorff, points out that the more bizarre an idea, the more arousing it is, the more memorable it is, and the more unique it is. It stands out. Great ideas stand out. Take a Blue Slip and label it UNIQUE and write down what you see as unique about your partner's Crazy Idea. What makes it stand out? Where does it have potential for greatness?

Step 7: Positive negativity

Now, start first with the positive (remember PIN?). Take a Blue Slip and label it ADVANTAGE and write down a possible advantage hidden in your partner's Crazy Idea.

Next consider the Crazy Idea from a "how to implement" angle. What limitations does the idea have that will raise questions? What roadblocks do you think it will run into? Note this is not a negative viewpoint; it is an effort to bring positive, focused critical analysis to the idea. Take a new Blue Slip, label it LIMITATIONS, and write down any major limitations you see, things that have been overlooked.

Step 8: Energizing ideas

Innovation starts with an idea and can also end there. To move from a creative idea to an innovation, there must be action. The idea must be implemented. As Peter Drucker once pointed out, "All ideas must degenerate into work if

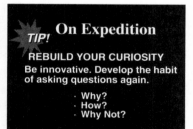

TIP! **On Expedition**
REBUILD YOUR CURIOSITY
Be innovative. Develop the habit of asking questions again.
· Why?
· How?
· Why Not?

anything is to happen." Imagine that you were given the job of implementing your partner's Crazy Idea. Take a Blue Slip and label it STEP #1 and write down the first step you would take to get this idea moving—not fully implemented, just energized. Then assume that STEP #1 has been done, what would STEP #2 be? Write it down, too.

Step 9: Fast-forward clarification

Now you're ready to have a clarifying, structured discussion. This will be broken into two stages: your Crazy Idea and your partner's Crazy Idea. Choose one of the two Crazy Ideas and take two minutes each to first explain 1) what you saw as unique and novel; 2) what advantages you found and what was useful about it; and 3) what limitations the idea had, and what you felt was missing in the idea.

This is a listening exercise. While one of you is reading his or her thoughts from the Blue Slips, the other should try to listen as intently as possible. Don't think about what you are going to say when it's your turn; instead, paraphrase what your partner just said. Take turns reading your Blue Slips and listening.

Step 10: Action planning

When you've finished sharing all of the Blue Slips, discuss the possibility the ideas have for implementation. Then jointly, as a team, come up with two more Blue Slips with action steps for moving the idea toward reality. Label these Blue Slips STEP #3 and STEP #4.

Clip all of the Blue Slips for each idea together in the following order:

MESS
CRAZY
NOVEL
UNIQUE
ADVANTAGE
USEFUL
LIMITATIONS
MISSING
STEPS #1, #2, #3, #4 (or more)

Turns a Crazy Idea into a concept

116

Take a blank Blue Slip, label it NAME and come up with a catchy name that capitalizes on the novelty or uniqueness of your partner's Crazy Idea. Clip the NAME Blue Slip on the top of the appropriate stack. Then start over again with your partner's crazy idea.

You have now converted two Crazy Ideas into concepts with shape and action plans. You've also expanded your normal thinking into the realm of impossible. Approximately 20 percent of the ideas produced with this technique can lead to near-term breakthrough improvements!

Risky Prospect Day

In July of 1988, while I was working exclusively with Exxon Company, USA, we ran an Innovation Briefing for Dave Lehman, a manager in the Central Production Division. This was one of the first innovation sessions outside of Exxon's Marketing Department, where my work had begun, and Francesco Corona, a young field engineer, hit on the Crazy Idea of drilling riskier prospects as a way to overcome bottlenecks in production operations. During the Innovation Briefing he kept writing the idea down on Blue Slips from a variety of perspectives. Many of them were connected to the perception that management simply would not take risks or that management was too stubborn to try new concepts. The more ideas Francesco had about this, the more he began to focus on considering deeper and riskier plays in mature oil fields.

Dave Lehman jumped on the idea, and on August 30, one month after the Innovation Briefing, "Risky Prospect Day" became a reality. Dave's assessment of the perception (as part of management) was that to his knowledge not a single well that had been presented to management had ever been turned down—and that they were simply not being brought to management's attention for fear of being turned down. Dave asked that a Technical Review, called Risky Prospect Day, be held and that management then look at the riskiest prospects for drilling that the various production geologists were aware of. He further offered to

buy lunch for any geologist who could show him a legitimate prospect that was too risky to endorse.

Further, the geologists as much as possible would do their analyses at the "back of an envelope" level. Dave's requirements for the prospects:

1. geologic map presentation describing the play concept
2. any additional data to support the idea
3. estimate of reserve potential
4. probable drill costs (optional)
5. a limit of fifteen to twenty minutes for the presentation

Eleven Risky Prospects were reviewed, six were worked up for formal presentation, and one was to be worked up as soon as additional seismic data was acquired. Four prospects were in fact labeled too risky for Exxon to drill, and three of those were recommended to be promoted as farmouts. Three lunches were bought and paid for the next day by Dave Lehman, and Risky Prospect Day was a big success. The first well drilled came in at a level that proved the concept!

The major benefits were not so much in the successful drilling but more in the creation of a forum for engineers and geologists to show their riskier thinking to management for evaluation prior to extensive workup and preparation for formal committee presentations—without the demoralizing effect of having an idea "turned down" publicly. The geologists later progressed to in-house workshops and seminars in which they shared skills and techniques for looking at Risky Prospects in very different ways, usually converting them into Risky Prospects, NOT by drawing on the diversity of their pooled expertise.

Crushing Without Crushing
In 1995, I ran a Thinking Expedition for Battelle National Laboratories, which does R & D contract work strictly for the government. The Expedition focused on the problem of disposing three million tons of napalm, which the U.S. Navy

had stockpiled in Southern California. The napalm was stored in aluminum containers, and the navy wanted them crushed. The project was behind schedule. One Crazy Idea got it back on track. What can't be done? What if the containers were crushed without crushing them, without having to make the machinery that pounds them flat? Impossible. Yet, the cylinders could be "crushed" by evacuating the air in them. When you pump out all of the air, atmospheric pressure crushes the cylinders. This idea and several other engineering design ideas accelerated the project by a number of months and helped put it back on schedule.

ROLF'S THEORY OF RELATIVITY

This is the shakiest level of change when it comes to relativity. It's the one you will most likely get an argument on because people's levels of knowledge are different and so their interpretation of what's impossible is different. Also, depending upon whether someone is a strong adapter (Level 1, 2, or 3 thinker—effectiveness, efficiency, improving) or a strong innovator (Level 5, 6 or 7 thinker—copying, different, impossible), that person's interpretation of impossible will be very different. What is an impossible change to a Level 1 person may be a simple efficiency change to a Level 7 person.

The relativity here has a lot to do with: How do you know what you don't know if you don't know you don't know?

THINKING ABOUT THINKING

Level 7 thinking is imaginative thinking. It's the formation of a mental image of something that is neither perceived as real nor present to the senses. Imaginative thinking is the ability to confront or deal with reality by using the creative power of the mind—resourceful thinking.

Level 7 thinking is breakout thinking. It's thinking that overcomes obstacles or restrictions. It's a thinking process that penetrates a paradigm's lines of defense. Level 7 thinking leads to a major idea or successful concept that permits further progress, as in new technology. It's forceful thinking that pushes through and emerges from a restrictive mental condition or perceived situation.

Better

What could we do better?
How could we do it better?

...BLUE SLIP

MINDSHIFT

The mindshift necessary to think at Level 7 is into imagining things that can't possibly happen. The single biggest mindshift you can make is total suspension of judgment. As soon as you say impossible, you are judging. When you suspend judgment, anything's possible. To make this mindshift you have to be willing to play with ideas instead of rejecting or immediately embracing them. Thinking at Level 7 is childlike thinking—it's naive and forever questioning.

This is the edge of the envelope—3-Sigma thinking—as different as it gets. Break out. The impossible, the unlikely, the uncomfortable. Consider the following diagram. To do things that can't be done, you have to break out of normal patterns of thinking. To break out, you have to think imaginatively.

| LEVEL 7: IMPOSSIBLE! | DO THINGS THAT CAN'T BE DONE | BREAKOUT IMAGINATIVE THINKING |

LEVEL 7 PROS & CONS

When you have a Level 7 idea and it comes to fruition, it often carries with it the mark of genius. The positives are incredible change—you've achieved the impossible, and with it can come fame and wealth and incredible success.

But there's a fine line between genius and insanity! You may have to generate fifty ideas to get one breakthrough—and Level 7 thinkers often do. Unfortunately, despite the breakthrough, people will remember the weird ideas among the fifty as well as the breakthrough—and how uncomfortable they were with them. You can't look crazy if everyone around you isn't suspending judgment or isn't willing to play with ideas.

There's a lot of risk to Level 7 ideas because beyond Level 6 (different), you're in new territory. There's no historical perspective. There's nothing to connect back to, nor anything similar to compare against. And anytime you do compare it with something, you're going against long-established, proven ways of dealing with something. The biggest roadblocks are

120

not in the technology challenges but in the perception of what is possible. You're frequently shattering something a lot of people have believed in. That's a powerful mindshift that some people simply can't handle. There's fallout. You may be eliminating people. People may quit because the change is so radical. The impact of change at this level is huge and has the potential of being unmanageable. You're on the far side of 3-Sigma—impossible thinking.

You're on expedition. You're exploring. You're moving into the unknown, and some people won't want to come along. Others are sorry they went.

ME, INC.®

At Level 7 you break out of the past and shift into your future—the impossible dreams and far-off summits that lie beyond the horizons of your goals and values, abilities, strengths, and skills. By going through this process of mentally incorporating, you can emerge with a new attitude toward change. Mentally incorporating yourself will change the way you think about yourself, and, in the process, it will open up pathways of change that will become a new vision of yourself.

Think of the impossible. Push the envelope and stretch. "Wouldn't it be great if…" Make a wish. Make more. Where do you see yourself, and what do you want to become in five or ten or twenty years? Write your wish down as a first step to getting there.

TRANSITION TO WHAT'S NEXT

So what happens beyond impossible? Where do you go when you've done what you didn't think you could do? If your goal is continuous improvement, you start the whole process again back at the beginning. You take the impossible, your Level 7 idea, and you implement it as doing the right thing—effectiveness (Level 1); then you do it more efficiently (Level 2); you improve it (Level 3); you do away with parts of it you now find you don't need (Level 4, cutting); you look outward and copy things other people are doing that can make it better (Level 5); you make it different (Level 6); and then you're back to impossible (Level 7) again.

1 - Sigma Change

Effective - Doing the right things
Efficient - Doing things right
Improving - Doing things better

Of course, every idea won't go through each level, but you can easily see how once you've done the impossible, you have to start over somewhere if you are going to continue to be innovative.

Breakthroughs don't stay breakthroughs very long.

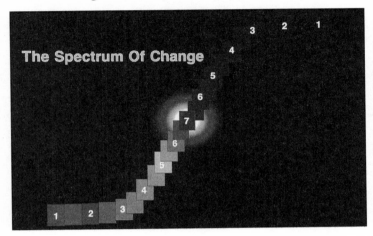

The Spectrum Of Change

Breakthroughs create strategic inflection points where everything shifts on the spectrum of change...

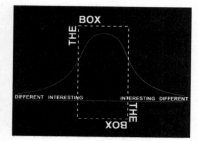

WHAT'S NEXT?

Every ending is also a beginning. If you are going to succeed at continuous improvement, you have to be continuously innovative, and that means continuous change. Change doesn't start with a new beginning. It starts when you let go of the way you used to do something—the ending.

What do you do when your wish comes true, when you achieve the impossible? You can't stop because you can bet that someone is already copying (Level 5) you right now. You've done the impossible—suddenly it's not impossible. You can't just stop changing if you are truly going to be innovative.

When you've achieved the impossible, you need to come up with a new vision to carry you forward. Think about the Berlin Wall. I remember talking to my wife's uncle, Horst Hirsch, a Berliner, in 1989. He'd been a sixteen-year-old German soldier during the fall of Berlin in World War II. He later saw the Russians put up the Berlin Wall, and he knew it was a permanent reality. It would never come down. He just knew that the Soviet Union would never let that happen. "*Nicht möglich.*" Impossible.

From his point of view, the wall would always be there. Germany would never be reunited. The Soviet empire would last forever. Two months after our conversation, the wall came down. Today, all of that stuff is ho-hum. The entire Eastern block is busy reinventing itself beyond impossible.

Tip!
Level 7 doesn't stay Level 7 very long.

Level 7 is Level 6. It's only Level 7 while you're at Level 7 thinking, while you think it's impossible. Once you shift to doing and implementing the change, it's not impossible anymore—you just did it, so now it's only different. It has instantly moved down to Level 6. What was impossible isn't. Think about it!

WHAT'S NEXT TOOL #1: BEYOND IMPOSSIBLE

Don't wait! After you've done something big, something really different or impossible—and you have it working—it's not what it was. Now it's out there, subject to straightforward Level 5 copying and adapting by your competitors. And when you find yourself thinking about that, it's your inner signal to mindshift to beyond impossible. I'm not ready to call it Level 8 yet, but it is a change, and it means it's time to get off the curve you're on and jump on another.

124

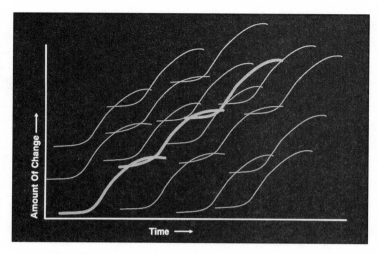

Don't ride your Level 7 idea all the way back down to Level 1 or 2 or 3 where you can bog down in making it more effective or efficient or in trying to improve it. Look at where you are, look at the height you've reached, and consider the new perspective you now have with this Level 7 breakthrough idea of yours. Use that for leverage, draw on all the smaller Level 2, 3, 4, 5, and 6 thinking you did to position yourself to reach Level 7. Start looking for places where you can set up a new high camp, a new position from which you can break out and find a different route to new summits, to new and different areas to explore. And then do it again—and again, and again.

Tip!

"Keep Moving Forward—KMF—beyond impossible!"
Chuck Grey

LEVEL 4
Cutting

Stopping Doing Things

THINKING BEYOND IMPOSSIBLE

If all of this makes you exhausted, if you can't handle any more change, if the rate of change coming at you is overpowering, then move beyond impossible. *Change* change.

That concept hit me very hard a few years ago while I was talking with an army brigadier general, the chief of staff at Fort Hood, Texas. He raised it as a challenge. "We can't take any more change," he said. "We've gone through reengineering, downsizing, TQM, budget cuts, and a war [Iraq]. We've cut the fat, and we've given all the blood we can—and now it's down to bone and tissue. We've got to get hold of change. We've got to *change* change!"

BAM! What a thought. *Change* change? How?

What if—we viewed the 7 Levels of Change as having an underlying mathematical basis? What if—we viewed change as a mathematical function, an expression of laws of physics and dynamics: I knew from all the work we'd been doing with the 7 Levels that the relationships between the changes—the delta or change between each of the changes themselves—is not a straight line progression or extrapolation.

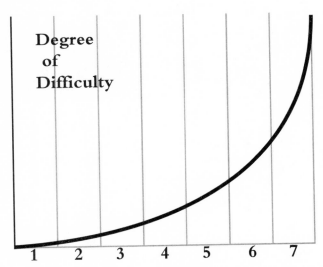

So I looked at physics. The simplest form of change is a change of position: moving from point A to point B. The next is speed, the rate of change of position. That is followed by acceleration, change of change of position. With that in mind, I reflected on the thinking of some great minds (Level 5

126

copying) and hit on a hypothesis: The energy (e) required to make a particular change is equal to the mindshift (m) needed times the square of the level of change (c) being made.

$$e = mc^2$$

The mindshift relates to the change in thinking that correlates to the particular level of change. How to *change* change? What if we took the square root of change! That would flatten the upward ramping curve of change into a flat line. It would convert the exponential aspects of change to a straight line relationship.

WHAT'S NEXT TOOL #2: OOTCHING

How to change change for nonmathematicians? Return to baseline. After each major change, touch back to the lower levels—Level 1—Effectiveness; Level 2—Efficiency; Level 3—Improving. And on your way up, employ the highly technical tool of "ootching," which means shifting up increasingly steep slopes from level to level in small increments. Ootching is a term I picked up while working on strategic redirection with David Messner, at the time the corporate strategic thinker for E-Systems, a high-tech defense firm in Dallas. David was a U.S. Air Force Academy graduate and Harvard MBA, and he is one of the sharpest and deepest thinkers I know. He used ootching to describe the way a lot of ideas and concepts were

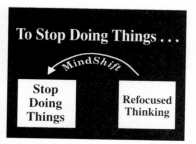

developed at E-Systems, and the word instantly connected for me. It says it all relative to change.

How fast can you make an ending, transition through the neutral zone—the vacuum the ending creates—and move on into a new beginning is all part of what makes each level what it is. It's easier for most people to make those lower level changes more quickly. The higher you get, the more ootching may be required. And thinking differently is ootching—the square root of change.

ME, INC.®

You're almost finished with your mental incorporation. Now all you need is an action plan to ootch you toward your vision. There are a number of underpinnings that must be in place to support your future. These are Critical Success Factors (CSFs)—things that either must or need to be in place for you to succeed. Try to limit yourself to no more than seven CSFs. None of them should contain the word "and," making them compound statements. Separate any compound thoughts into two CSFs. Each should contain the words "must" or "need." A must is necessary and means you cannot accomplish your goal without it. A need is important, and if you don't have it, your goal will be difficult to reach (Levels 3, 4, and 6 thinking). These CSFs form the baseline for determining your strategies.

Consider some broad strategies to follow as you carry out your mission, for accomplishing your goals, for leveraging your strengths, values, and principles to move you toward your vision (Levels 3, 4, 5, and 6 thinking).

Then move from strategic thinking to action thinking. Ask yourself, "What are the steps I need to take now to succeed?" And keep in mind that while you are creating your vision, you are moving up the 7 Levels of Change. As you create your action steps, most often you are moving back down.

Now that you have put yourself through the entire Me, Inc.® process, look back at your work, edit, condense, and refine. For a complete recap of the process, read the Me, Inc.® appendix in the back of this book. Use the one-page

*C*ritical
*S*uccess
*F*actors

128

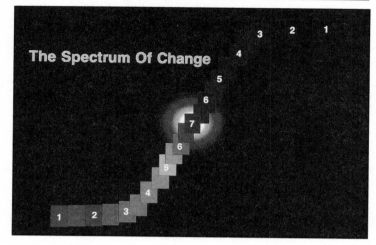

form that's in the back of the book to describe yourself—Me, Inc.® Cut it out (it has a front and back side) and transcribe all your work onto it. It folds up to the size of a business card because that's what it is—a Level 6 business card—YOU as a business. Carry it with you in your wallet or purse, and when you feel like you're off track, use it as a reminder to refocus and motivate. Pull it out and explain yourself to people you meet—who you are, what your purpose and mission are, where you're going. Then ask them for some ideas!

KMF! Don't stop changing. Check your progress. Reevaluate yourself regularly. Rethink. Reinvent Me, Inc.®

GETTING READY FOR CHANGE

In the process of working with teams on Thinking Expeditions and with individuals in the School for Innovators, we've discovered some strong correlations between thinking style, problem-solving style, learning style, personality type, and degree of comfort with the various levels of change. Our work has led to some interesting insights into how people view change and deal with change.

As part of preparing for a Thinking Expedition or attending the School for Innovators, everyone completes the Kirton Adaption-Innovation (KAI) Inventory and the Myers-Briggs Type Indicator (MBTI). These inventories are based on differing but broadly related theories of cognitive processes. The KAI defines differences in creative style (thinking), and the MBTI defines differences in personality type (behavior).

The inventories give us multiple vectors of insight and leverage points around which we shape and customize the approach, content, and flow of a Thinking Expedition.

CREATIVE STYLE

We're interested in creative style because it tells us how a person deals with solving problems. We've found that it is also a strong indicator of how people are likely to view and deal with change.

Adaption-Innovation theory has roots that date back to 1961, and work done by Michael Kirton in observing organizational behavior as well as to an early paper relating to an inventory developed by Kirton in 1976. Kirton's studies of organizations going through major change reflected, in many cases, substantial delays in the introduction of change and objections to new ideas as well as the rejection of suggestions by certain managers who were perceived to be "outside" of the establishment. Kirton believes that such resistance to change is independent of the abilities and intelligence of the individuals involved and much more related to the creative styles of the managers and differences in thinking.

In our work we find this to be true again and again and have found the Kirton Adaption-Innovation (KAI) Inventory to be extremely useful. KAI theory helps us define and measure an individual's characteristic style of decision making and problem solving. According to the theory, everyone can be rated on a one-dimensional continuum

130

OBSERVATION

KAI is a measure of style, not level or ability or intelligence!

LEVELS of CHANGE

7

6

5

4

3

2

1

0

ADAPTIVE INNOVATIVE

Sometimes innovation may just be a matter of getting rid of something

of scores ranging from highly adaptive (those who solve problems within an existing system) to highly innovative (those who solve problems by challenging the norms of the system).

The KAI Inventory is a simple, one-page form of thirty-two questions that yields a total KAI score which can range from 32 (extreme adaptor) to 160 (extreme innovator). The scores are distributed normally over the general population with a mean of 96. The KAI Inventory is a measure of style and not level or ability.

Generally speaking, the more strongly adaptive the score, the less comfortable the person tends to be with change and, in the extreme, is actually resistant to change. The more strongly innovative the score, the more inclined the person is likely to seek out change or to function as a change agent, leading the way to change. In the extreme, the innovator is often interested in change just for the sake of change.

There appears to be a correlation between KAI scores and the 7 Levels of Change. Strong adaptors will focus on Levels 1, 2, and 3 (effectiveness, efficiency, and improving). Their operative change words are "better" and "improve." Midrange adaptors will connect well with the concept of continuous improvement, moving into 2-Sigma thinking at Level 4 (cutting) to eliminate waste. Typically, adaptors will protect the status quo and try to work within the existing system.

The midrange innovator will essentially start thinking about change at Level 4 (cutting). But such an innovator will do it with more of a focus on stopping doing things that don't make sense in order to make room to copy and adapt (Level 5) something interesting. This would involve adapting something they've seen someone else doing that will lead to effectiveness and efficiency.

When strong innovators think at Level 4 (cutting), they want to blow it all up and start from scratch. Their tendency is to use Level 5 change to copy something different in order to get a big change in place sooner and to more easily justify it for their more adaptive teammates ("Look, these guys are doing it, and it works for them," they'll say). Their natural bias is toward 3-Sigma thinking, the new and different or Level 6 change. They continuously push their thinking into Level 7, generating a lot of unusual, off-the-wall, extreme, and crazy ideas that occasionally turn into a really BIG change. In general, innovators will attack the status quo and try to bring in ideas from outside the system.

Adaptors and innovators, looking at exactly the same change from their respective sides of the KAI fence, will often see the same thing as a very different level of change. The innovators will tend to minimize the implications of the scope and level of a change, while the adaptors will maximize the implications of its scope and impact. Thus, an innovator may see some particular change as a simple improvement (Level 3 change) while the adaptor might see it as radically different (Level 6) or, in the extreme, as a change that is impossible to implement in the organization (Level 7).

Two different views of reengineering might be:

Innovator: Reengineering = "kill all the managers"

Adaptor: Reengineering = "cut fat and eliminate waste"

PERSONALITY TYPE

The Myers-Briggs Type Indicator® (MBTI) is another instrument we have found extremely useful in understanding how people view and deal with change. It provides a second vector of perspective that complements the KAI very well. The MBTI is a forced-choice inventory that operationalizes much of Carl Jung's theory of individual differences in human behavior or type. There are several accepted variations of the inventory with between 84 and 122 questions. The MBTI takes twenty to thirty minutes to complete, and a basic feedback session requires an hour or two.

Myers-Briggs theory and the use of the MBTI is complex and not something that is quickly understood and easily applied. The apparent simplicity of the various types, described in four-letter combinations, can be misleading.

Style KAI ≠ Type MBTI

132

However, in the context of understanding human behavior around change, it's well worth studying.

Jung developed a comprehensive theory to explain human personality based on patterns in behavior. He referred to these patterns as "psychological types" and used them to classify the way people prefer to take in information (perceive things) and how they organize the information once they've taken it in (how they make judgments).

Jung classified all conscious mental activity into four processes or functions—two perception processes and two judgment processes. The perception processes are sensing and intuition, and the judgment processes are thinking and feeling. His theory was that anything that comes into the conscious mind does so either through the senses or through intuition. Then, for perceived things to stay in the conscious mind, they must be used, so the judgment processes—thinking and feeling—sort, compare, weigh, analyze, and evaluate them.

The MBTI gives people insights into their functions and attitudes, identifying sixteen different patterns possible through the four pairs of preferences that follow Jung's theory.

The perceiving processes are the driver of Jung's model. Sensing (S on the MBTI grid) is the term used for perceiving concrete things by using the senses—sight, touch, smell, taste, hearing. Intuition (N on the MBTI grid) is the term used for perceiving abstract things such as meanings, relationships, and possibilities through insight.

Sensing (S) types want to start with what is known and real—solid ground—relying on actual experience and proven results, not theory. They trust the conventional way of doing things and like simplicity. It is from this kind of mental baseline that they explore outward—systematically, step-by-step, linking each new idea back into past experience and forward into relevant, practical applications. Their focus tends to be the current and the now, using sound, conventional wisdom. They approach change slowly, carefully, incrementally—and critically. Sensing types are the most resistant to change.

Intuitive (N) types like complexity and theoretical relationships and connections between things. They have the

S → Most Resistant to change

IF IT'S DUMB
IT'S NOT OUR POLICY

What are we doing that's dumb?

...BLUE SLIP

ability to see future possibilities, often unusual and abstract ones, using imagination and theory. They rely on inspiration rather than past experience and learn through an intuitive grasp of meanings and relationships, skipping steps and often making apparent leaps between new ideas. They have strong interests in the untried, the new, and the unknown, and are motivated by intellectual challenge. They approach change openly and optimistically, preferring larger-scale, fundamental jumps to incremental steps. Intuitive types are the most receptive to change.

Thinking (T on the MBTI grid) is the term used for the process of logical and impersonal decision making. Feeling (F on the MBTI grid) is the term used for arriving at conclusions through a process of appreciation employing a system of subjective personal values.

Feeling (F) types develop personal values and standards, and a subjective knowledge of what matters most to themselves and other people. The attitudes they develop typically reflect a warm understanding of people, compassion, empathy, and a need for harmony.

Thinking (T) types apply logical analysis to allow them to weigh facts and examine consequences objectively. They develop attitudes of impartiality, a sense of fairness and justice, and tough-minded objectivity.

A third personality dimension, which Jung identified, deals with how people get personal energy and how they act in their environment. Jung chose the terms "extroversion" and "introversion" to label these attitudes and defined the terms much more broadly than their normal, everyday usage. Unfortunately, because people therefore confuse the terms with traits commonly associated with "extrovert" and "introvert," real effort is required to ensure clear understanding of the words as attitudes.

The extroverted (E on the MBTI grid) attitude focuses outward from self and has a higher awareness of the environment it relies on for stimulation and direction. Extroverted types are action oriented and tend to be impulsive ("when in doubt, act"). They communicate easily and

[handwritten margin notes: INTuitive (N) → most open to change; T/F: How we make decisions: objective vs. subjective basis]

134

literally think out loud, throwing out half-thought and incomplete ideas in an almost constant stream. For them, things often don't make sense until after they say them. As a result, they are seen as more outgoing and sociable. Someone sitting next to an extroverted type on an airline flight will get off the plane knowing virtually everything there is to know about the person; anything they don't know is simply because they weren't listening.

The introverted (I on the MBTI grid) attitude focuses inward into self and the inner world of concepts, ideas, and thoughts. As a result, they are thoughtful, contemplative, reflective ("when in doubt, think about things more deeply"), and they enjoy privacy and quiet time alone. Introverted types keep their half-baked ideas inside, examining them and working on them mentally until they are fully done and ready to be exposed. The person sitting next to an introverted type on an airplane will have a quiet, undisturbed trip and at the end will know very little of a personal nature about him or her. Anything they don't know about the person will be a function of their not having specifically asked. Introverted types are typically seen as being uncommunicative and more reserved socially.

In the process of developing the MBTI, Isabel Myers and Katherine Briggs added a fourth dimension to Jung's model of psychological type—attitude toward the outer world in which people find themselves or the manner in which they run their lives. This attitude defines how people actually apply the perceiving functions (sensing/intuition) and the judging functions (thinking/feeling) to their lives. Myers and Briggs defined this attitude as judging (J) and perceiving (P).

The judging attitude is convergent, always driving toward closure and results and toward having a system or systems to work within. When a person favors a judging process (thinking or feeling), things are organized, scheduled, settled, and managed by plans and priorities. As a result, the judging attitude is not particularly keen on change.

The perceiving attitude is divergent, open, flexible, and unconstrained. When a perception process (sensing or feeling) is used, the natural bias is to keep things open to new and more perceptions and possibilities as long as possible. The

J/P → How we run our lives

LEVEL 4 CHANGE

Streamlining

perceiving type doesn't want to miss experiencing anything. His or her tendency is to minimize plans, organization, rules, and structure to adapt freely to changing circumstances.

The judging/perceiving aspect of a person's life is often the first element of their type that we notice as we get to know them to any degree. It is difficult even for a strong introvert not to disclose through behavior whether he or she is spontaneous or organized.

These eight characteristics in their corresponding four preference combinations define Myers-Briggs types. How those combinations are arrived at is shown with the corresponding pairs below:

Extroversion	E ←→ I	Introversion
Sensing	S ←→ N	Intuition
Thinking	T ←→ F	Feeling
Judging	J ←→ P	Perceiving

These preferences in turn create sixteen possible combinations, traditionally arranged in a matrix as below:

ISTJ	ISFJ	INFJ	INTJ
ISTP	ISFP	INFP	INTP
ESTP	ISFP	INFP	INTP
ESTJ	ESFJ	ENFJ	ENTJ

Recent MBTI research [Allen Hammer and Wayne Mitchell, *Journal of Psychological Type*, Vol. 37, 1996] reveals that:

- Thirty-seven percent of people fall in the IS Quadrant and are referred to as "detail oriented."
- Thirty-one percent of people fall in the ES Quadrant and are referred to as "pragmatists."
- Fifteen percent of people fall in the IN Quadrant and are referred to as "academics."
- Seventeen percent of people fall in the EN Quadrant and are referred to as "innovators."

136

THE SPECTRUM OF CHANGE

When the basic attributes and functions (behaviors) are combined into the sixteen types and overlaid across the 7 Levels of Change, we have seen some strong patterns relating to change. When combined with the percentage distribution data, we can make some powerful generalizations about relative strength of resistance and receptivity to change and at what levels of change:

Sensing (S) is the most broadly resistive factor to change (68 percent of people).

Intuition (N) is the most broadly receptive factor to change (32 percent of people).

Judging (J) is the next most resistive factor to change (63 percent of people).

Perceiving (P) is the next most receptive factor to change (37 percent of people).

Feeling (F) is the third strongest factor in resistance to change (48 percent of people)

Thinking (T) is the third most receptive factor to change (52 percent of people).

Introversion (I) is last in effect on resistance to change (53 percent of people)

Extroversion (E) is last in effect on receptivity to change (47 percent of people).

SO WHAT?

The diagram below conceptually shows the relative strength by type of both resistence to change and receptivity to change, overlaid on the spectrum of the 7 Levels of Change. The change "resistence-acceptance line of demarcation" this highlights raises some interesting hypotheses.

The Pareto Principle
[The 80:20 Rule]

80% of the results come from 20% of the efforts

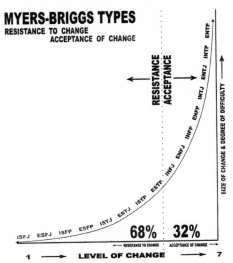

MYERS-BRIGGS TYPES
RESISTANCE TO CHANGE
ACCEPTANCE OF CHANGE

We can generalize from this then and hypothesize that "normal behavior" is to resist change. Sensing = 68 percent = 1-Sigma. That is to say that two-thirds of all people resist change. Further, that nearly half of all people will tend to strongly resist change (46 percent SJs). About one-third (the remaining 32 percent NJs and NTJs) will be receptive to change ("interesting" 2-Sigma behavior), while only 10 percent (the NTPs) will be strongly receptive to change and act as change agents (3-Sigma "different" behavior).

Resisting or accepting change is clearly not an even split, and the challenge of rolling out change can be even more appreciated with this in mind. "Typing" a team and "typing" the target group the change is going to be dropped on makes a good case for using a tool like the 7 Levels of Change to help people better understand and deal with change in the context of who they are and how they are likely to react.

GETTING READY FOR CHANGE TOOL #1: TYPING TEAMS

Teams are well worth "typing," and the team's type is not a simple sum of its individual team members' types. By determining a team's dominant attitudes and spotting its "holes" in terms of both attitudes and types early, a number of difficulties

This is a real "wow!" for most people

Tip! Look for big type "holes" in a Team

138

can be anticipated and planned for, and the design of the processes to be used with the team can be shaped according-ly. One size does not fit all. The end effect is nearly always a compression in the time it takes the team to come together and bond, and correspondingly, the time the team needs to get into breakout thinking and high value results.

Much of our experience in working with organizations and change has been at the team level, where the team is focused on a particularly unusual or urgent problem, using the format of a Thinking Expedition. This tends to inten-sify experiences as well as both compress and accelerate the time frames, highlighting individual and team type in the process.

One of our most interesting Thinking Expeditions in terms of creative style and psychological type being key success fac-tors was one jointly sponsored by Proctor & Gamble and Honeywell. The challenges they had agreed to focus on were all tied to communication, mutual understanding, conflict res-olution, and strategic alignment of common objectives.

Classifying teams by their most dominant behavior (MBTI "attitudes") and their creative style in approaching problems (KAI style) are the first steps in looking at their change fac-tor—how they will function at the various levels of change and with the corresponding mindshifts in thinking.

Interestingly, the KAI scores of the two teams led us into drawing even more heavily than normal on the MBTI infor-mation. The composite KAI scores of the two-company team following a normal distribution, ranging from mid-range Adaptor to mid-range Innovator - ideal for problem-solving. However the average of each company's individual half of the team were widely different with a 30-point spread (raw score) between them - a 2-Sigma difference! Normally, a difference of 5 points in <u>team</u> averages can cause commu-nications difficulties, and 10 points real working difficulties; further, there was no overlap in the end scores of one team with those of the other. The two teams were very different.

The P&G team members were biased toward the adap-tive, and the Honeywell team members strongly toward the innovative.

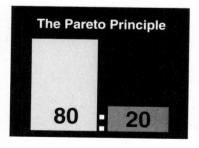

The Pareto Principle

80 : 20

In terms of type, the P&G team was essentially STJ (sensing-thinking-judging), and the Honeywell team appeared to be ENTP (extroverted-intuitive-thinking-perceiving). They were pretty much opposites with the exception of their thinking behavior. When we broke out the individual types, P&G owned the four corners, the classic executive/supervisor and engineer types, and Honeywell sat solidly in the classic innovator/inventor spots. One side was going to be driving for details, practical results, and no bells and whistles; the other side was going to be talking big picture concepts, new technologies, and possibilities. The P&G engineers were going to approach change and new systems slowly, carefully, and incrementally, and the Honeywellers were going to be pushing the conceptual and technological change envelope.

THE CHANGE FACTOR IN TEAMS AND ORGANIZATIONS

So, let's look at change teams and organizations. William Bridges, in his book *The Character of Organizations*, classifies organizations by type and highlights how each type of organization deals with change. The book is a useful reference for anyone either introducing change or working with change in an organization. Bridges has developed an inventory that he calls the "Organizational Character Index," which is similar to the MBTI but focused on organizational type. We've found it helpful for teams who are going to be rolling out major change into their organization.

SENSING TEAMS focus on the present and reality and believe in making only step-by-step, incremental change. They are good at fixing, remodeling, or enhancing how things are already being done and can always make something better, including the team itself. They do not look particularly far ahead. They become disoriented and confused if there are no clear transition procedures. They do best with Level 1, 2, and 3 changes (effectiveness, efficiencies, and improvements). Level 4 changes (stopping doing things or cutting things out) are a pretty good conceptual stretch for them. Sensing behavior as a type is the most dominant in resisting change.

SENSING TEAMS
← incremental change

140

INTUITIVE TEAMS
- 3-Sigma, BIG Change
- Most receptive to change

New ideas, trends, shifts

JUDGING TEAMS
Effective implementers of change

PERCEIVING TEAMS
want dramatic change!

INTUITIVE TEAMS are excited by change and move the most quickly. They are much more likely to see the big changes (3-Sigma) that lie ahead but don't see problems right in front of them. They believe that you need an overall design to integrate the whole project and in big, all-at-once changes in which the whole system is transformed. Their focus is on the possibilities that are under the surface of many situations. They are far more aware of new ideas, trends, shifts, and factors that sensing organizations will not recognize for months. They do well with visionary Level 6 and 7 changes (different and impossible) as well as more radical Level 4 changes (not just cutting but blowing things up!). Intuition is the behavior type most receptive to change.

JUDGING TEAMS look at change as a disruptive interruption or passing storm in what is otherwise a natural state of stability. They are uncomfortable with change and hunker down until the storm has passed when they will again be on solid, unchanging ground. Once they have bought in on the need for the change, they are the most effective at implementing it. They risk moving too quickly in an effort to get change over with fast, and once in execution they are difficult to redirect. Because they favor order and stability, they do best with Level 1, 2, and 3 changes (effectiveness, efficiency, and simple improvements) aimed at making things even more stable. Overall, judging behavior runs a close second to sensing in resisting change. They just don't like it because it messes things up.

PERCEIVING TEAMS are more likely to see change as the norm and stability as boring. They have little discomfort with change and respond easily to changing situations, going with the flow. Because they see an unchanging situation as unreal and inherently unstable, they tend to seek out and initiate more dramatic levels of change—Levels 4, 6, and 7 (killing sacred cows, the really new and different, and the impossible)—or motivate to copy (Level 5), a mind-boggling systemic change (Level 6 or 7) some other organization has implemented.

FEELING TEAMS are wary of change because of the unavoidable impact and disruption change has on people.

They are more likely to respond to the second order distress and disruptions that a change causes—the changes behind the change—than the basic change itself, and they often become engaged in change efforts which have something to do with organizational values. For the feeling team, logic and numbers are not the issue; the right thing to do is the humane thing. So changes that improve people's lives or working conditions (Level 3, improving), and changes which get rid of burdensome bureaucratic requirements (Level 4, cutting) appeal to them. However, most big, systemic organizational changes don't have those kinds of effects on people. Instead, they create stress and worry. Because of that, feeling teams are often strong resistors of change.

THINKING TEAMS approach any change or unexpected situation by almost reflexively applying logical analysis and sequential planning. For the thinking team, the right thing to do is the logical, effective thing, and the team will focus on ensuring that change leads to improved results. They look at a big change logically and simplistically and are able to see it as Level 1 change—doing the right thing. Thinking teams frequently initiate Level 4 change (stopping and cutting) since they are unlikely to continue a course of action that is not working well and simply cut their losses. They will do that even though such a change may impact the people involved. When planning change or rolling out change, thinking teams tend to overlook or downplay the fact that it is people who will have to implement change and make change work. With their logical perspective on change, thinking teams are able to mentally handle almost any level of change thrown at them. Logically, they think other people should be able to do that, too.

INTROVERTED TEAMS are slow to respond to change and sometimes actively resist responding to allow themselves some quiet time to figure things out and work out their responses completely. Because they are focused on and driven largely by their own internal processes and values, they

Thinking Teams
- Do the right thing
- cut losses

142

*EXTROVERTED TEAMS
— strongly receptive
to change*

tend not to stay particularly aware of external events. They are much more active in responding to internal change, especially shifts in thinking, belief structures, and value systems—things an extroverted team might not even notice.

EXTROVERTED TEAMS are in constant touch with what is happening around them, so when changes arise in their operating environment, they view them as normal events and are usually comfortable with them. They are relatively quick to respond to any external change and reorient themselves with little difficulty to create new connections with what is going on. They need to talk a lot about change and have a continuous flow of communication relating to it. Extroversion as a team attitude runs a strong second to Intuition in being receptive to change.

SO WHAT?

Back to the Proctor & Gamble/Honeywell Thinking Expedition for a quick look. While people from both Proctor & Gamble and Honeywell were frustrated with one another, the Thinking Expedition format got them all to the same place fast—diffferent. By learning more about one another through KAI and Myers-Briggs, both organizations began collaborating on ideas in a better way, fast—and developing creative solutions that would benefit both organizations. P&G would get global hardware and service at affordable prices and rates, and Honeywell would get higher volume and continuing business.

Today, both organizations—using many of the tools learned on Thinking Expedition, are developing common business objectives that will meet each organization's unique business needs as they both expand globally.

HOW THE 7 LEVELS LEAD TO INNOVATIVE CHANGE

It's time to get started with your own organization. The following generalities may help you take the first steps.

At the lower levels of change, smaller, more immediately useful and easily implemented ideas can be pursued by people who view themselves as more practical and conventional.

LEVEL 4 CHANGE

STOP

What can we stop doing?

...BLUE SLIP

Changes at these levels tend to be adaptive in nature, focusing on continuity with existing systems through incremental advances. Because they can be implemented relatively quickly, such changes are frequently "bottom line" oriented. They are typically perceived as "sound" improvements with relatively low risk/high stability factors. All of this combines to facilitate relatively easy acceptance of such changes by an organization.

People who view themselves as more progressive, nonconforming and conceptual in their thinking tend to conceive and advocate ideas at the higher levels of change where longer term, more far-reaching and potentially higher payoffs may evolve. The more such ideas move from the tactical toward the strategic, the more different original and pioneering the changes tend to be. Similarly, the higher the levels of change an organization participates in, the more it departs from conventional wisdom and tradition—with correspondingly higher perceived risks. Such higher level changes are not readily accepted by the organization and, in fact, are often resisted.

Simplistically, people have a natural tendency to approach tasks and problems in one of two ways: improvement versus different. Lower levels of change imply evolutionary improvements (incremental), while higher levels aim at very different, revolutionary (fundamental) advances.

Now, read on to The Thinking Expedition and see how six leading organizations did it!

Change

INCREMENTAL

Fine-tuning, sticking with things we are
Comfortable with but making small
improvements

FUNDAMENTAL

Results in a new way of doing our work-
Giving up some of the past which results
in a Quantum change in performance

THE
THINKING EXPEDITION

Some things just happen. However, the concept of the Thinking Expedition evolved deliberately. Since 1991, the School for Innovators has increasingly integrated mountaineering, rock-climbing, and expedition metaphors into the basic curriculum of thinking differently and Creative Problem Solving (CPS). The results have significantly stretched and changed our students. Our postgraduate feedback has been overwhelmingly positive.

What is an expedition? It's an excursion, a journey, or voyage made for an express purpose. It's an exploration of discovery into unknown regions to gain insight or knowledge of something previously unseen or unknown. An expedition is about different.

And how do you move through the 7 Levels of Change on expedition? In very predictable stages—take a look:

Level 1: Effectiveness—
Doing the right things

Learn what an expedition is, the basics of everything. Establish expectations. Meet the guide. Form up the team: Who's who? The Staging Area: procedures, rules, and roles. Learn where to focus, what to do—and why. Problem finding and planning. What to watch out for—dangers and safety. A lot of new "what."

Level 2: Efficiency—
Doing the right things right

Learn how to do things. New tools, techniques, processes. How to survive. How to discover and explore. How to find ideas. Developing basic expertise and a sense of mission. Expedition protocols and communication. Setting priorities. Charting a route. Crossing the frontier. Realizing. A lot of new "how."

Level 3: Improving—Doing things better

Having ideas. Learning new and better ways to be more efficient and effective. Acclimatizing to changes in the environment, altitude, weather, and people. The long trek into the interior. Issues and challenges. Setting up base camp. Mess finding and data finding. Building strengths. Becoming flexible.

Level 4: Cutting—Doing away with things

Letting go of old habits, perceptions, and preconceptions. 80:20 thinking and

---

The Thinking Expedition is a patented process, U.S. patent pending.

146

refocus, shedding unnecessary weight. Mindshifting, negative-positive tension. Moving to higher ground. Leaving base camp and comfortable behind. Leaner and meaner.

Level 5: Copying—
Doing things others are doing
Transitioning to out-of-the-box thinking. Knowing what you don't know. Observing and noticing. Copying and adapting what others know and do. The power of clipping in: pairs, triads, quads, small rope teams. Listening differently to yourself and others. Lateral thinking. Route finding—moving as small rope teams. Leapfrogging camps.

Level 6: Different—Doing things no one else is doing
Thinking differently. Experimenting, trying things. Reflecting, thinking up ideas. Creating new things out of old things, new ways of doing things. Exploring new ground. Shifting to climbing, risking differently. Path finding. Becoming a guide, leading teams. High camp.

Level 7: Impossible—Doing things that can't be done
Break out! Accelerating the rate of change, changing changes that have already occurred. Mindshifting beyond present rules, roles, and operations. Leveraging adversity, new and unexpected conditions. Higher-level barriers. The summit attempt. Discovering unknowns. Breakout and the impossible. Summiting. Descent and return. Bringing back results. The long trek home.

Following are six very different case studies of Thinking Expeditions I've led that will give you an idea of the incredible changes that can come from leaving home and the familiar, and setting off on an adventure with your mind.

FLETCHER WOOD PANELS, LTD., AUCKLAND, NEW ZEALAND

In January 1996, on very short notice, I found myself once again flying into an adventure in New Zealand.

CHANGE
Two Different Types

1st Order Change Change that occurs within a given system which itself remains unchanged

2nd Order Change Change whose occurence changes the system itself

Henry Osti, a principal with the Boston consulting firm of CSC/Index and a graduate of the School for Innovators (Expedition XIII, July 1994), had called me right after New Year's with an exciting, hair-on-fire, out-of-the-box idea... "and we can go rock climbing and scuba diving and hunting in the Southern Alps besides," he'd said at the end of his pitch. "It'll be an unbelievable expedition!"

It was late 1995, and somehow Henry was already in Auckland heading up a major re-creation project for Fletcher Wood Panels (FWP), one of the major operating divisions of Fletcher Challenge, a highly diversified New Zealand corporation. Fletcher Wood Panels had launched an initiative focused on the re-creation of their business—650 people in seven different locations. To make it happen, FWP entered into a strategic relationship with CSC/Index, a leading American reengineering consulting firm based in Boston, Massachusetts.

Henry, the CSC/Index project manager (since promoted to principal) had set the stage very differently for FWP with the theme of "On Expedition!" at a brief pre-Christmas kickoff meeting. I joined the team when it re-formed in January after the holidays. The team included some forty-two FWP employees and five CSC/Index reengineering consultants. Henry and I took the role of "lead guides," with Henry focusing on content and reengineering while I focused on thinking processes, thinking styles, psychological type, and teaming.

We snapped the group back to their pre-Christmas holidays framing by having everyone show up wearing expedition gear—hats, bush clothes, and boots—and set up the project team's main room as "base camp," decorated with camping equipment, ropes, packs, and maps. Meals were served in base camp in mess kits. (Imprinting everyone with "Hey, this is different!" is critical on a Thinking Expedition).

We opened the first meeting as a "nonmeeting," with no timelines for agenda items or schedule. As a result, no one felt concerned about having to know exactly what we had planned or what was supposed to happen when. The effect was that people quickly became comfortable with the high degree of ambiguity and unknown things that de facto

Imprinting "different"

"ENT" Team
Ready for BIG
3-Sigma Change!

KAI ξ MBTI →

2 - Sigma Thinking

INTERESTING

14%   14%

accompany re-creation/reengineering projects and Thinking Expeditions.

One of our basic rules was "No whining!" (suspend judgment). I showed the team video clips of Sir Edmund Hillary making the first successful climb of Mt. Everest in 1953, and wove clips from documentaries of several other famous mountain climbing and African expeditions into the 35mm slide presentation/workshop. The team immediately connected with the analogy, seeing the similarity between successful climbs and explorations and the expedition FWP was moving into. We highlighted the similarities that we would be capitalizing on: establishing a base camp of resources and support; teamwork and bonding; understanding and valuing individual differences and diversity of thinking, clearly defined roles, goals, and objectives; many unknowns; thorough preparation; and results (measurable successes).

In order to accelerate the mindshift into thinking about thinking, we issued every team member a Thinking Expedition Journal and taught them a variety of techniques to use with them. The journals were custom-designed for the FWP re-creation project using the School for Innovators' template. They contained the conceptual map of the expedition route and were prefaced with a joint letter from Colin Leach, managing director of FWP, and Heike Schicle, the FWP Team Project Manager, which laid out the charge, the mission, and broad direction for the team.

Colin's kickoff talk to the team also emphasized the importance of journal writing as a tool for team reflection and introspection, two processes that would be critical to keeping the team members aligned and focused on the changes they would work on together. At the start of each day, Henry or I led a short, ten-minute journaling session, focusing all team members on where they were and what they were learning and discovering in their explorations and efforts. It was followed by a brief Pair-And-Share exercise, a practice that quickly proved to be key to keeping everyone connected to what was happening.

The payoff was apparent quickly in the compressed rate at which the team was able to move into real work and visible results. Journaling is a basic Level 1 (Effectiveness) or Level 2 (Efficiency) tool on Thinking Expeditions. However, for the FWP team members, it was definitely a very different Level 6 change, a major mindshift.

Following are some of the more major stages of the FWP Thinking Expedition.

Level 1: (Effectiveness) and Level 2: (Efficiency) Changes

Using Think 101 tools, we next moved the team into basic idea finding and began the process of ingraining the habit of becoming aware of and capturing all the ideas that came up on the expedition. The team members were given packets of Blue Slips and trained to carry them at all times for idea capturing. By constantly asking questions relating to the re-creation project goals and having people write down their ideas, by the end of the first two weeks, the habit of capturing and playing with ideas was solidly formed. The team then transitioned from individual idea finding with Blue Slips to using them for rapid collection and processing of group feedback, focused on whatever problem or issue or new idea was at hand. Many of these ideas were turned into BIG Ideas, another J.I.T. idea-development tool, and rolled out to the manufacturing plants for "quick hits"—immediate implementation and immediate results.

Think 101 → Tools from School for Innovators

Level 3: (Improving) Meetings

At the end of each day, Blue Slips were used to run a "Hot Wash-up"—an on-the-spot critique of each day's progress, results, and things to do different (Level 3) the next day. This practice reinforced key points learned, personal insights, and group discoveries.

"Hot WASH-UP" every day
— Learnings
— Insights
— Discoveries

Level 5: Cultural Change

Today, Blue Slips and ideas have become a way of life in FWP, long past the completion of the re-creation project. FWP has since gone into "production" of Blue Slip packets, and they're a standard issue item in the company.

150

Team Dynamics

Big Hole...

**Doing Things
Others Are Doing**

More Level 6: (Different)

As Henry and I led the team deeper into the Thinking Expedition metaphor, we correspondingly moved them deeper into thinking about their own thinking processes and creative style. I grouped them into subteams and gave each team the mission of developing a visual representation of their vision for the re-creation project. They were also to highlight major issues and challenges and include the pros and cons, strengths and weaknesses of their particular subteam. They then re-formed in base camp, and the subteams debriefed the entire group with their results.

There were radical and very visible differences in content, approach, and presentation. At the end I explained that the subteams had been formed based on their scores on the Kirton Adaption-Innovation (KAI) Inventory (which everyone had completed prior to the kickoff session) so that the six subteams ranged from strong adapters to midrange adapters to midrange innovators to strong innovators. Their very diverse presentations were *almost* perfect examples of their KAI scores' creative style behaviors and characteristics. This set the backdrop for some intense work on Team Dynamics.

We began looking at personality type and the Myers-Briggs Type Indicator (MBTI) scores of the team. Once everyone was comfortable with their own type and had a good understanding of MBTI theory, we began to focus on Team Dynamics, using a variety of exercises tied to the actual re-creation work to help everyone look at the type composition of the overall team, each subteam, and the type/style of the CSC/Index consultants and the FWP subteam leaders. The team had some major holes—for example, there were only two "F" (feeling) types among the forty-seven people, and one of them was Henry. In addition, Henry's MBTI type and that of the FWP project manager were almost complete opposites—they had only one matching attribute. There were some very predictable tensions and challenges in a number of key aspects of the project!

More Level 6: (Different)

I spent quite a bit of time debriefing and coaching on style and type—first with the CSC/Index consultants as a team and then with each of the subteams. We went through KAI coping and flexing behavior and tools. Then we looked at each team through several lenses: leadership (temperament lens), change (quadrant lens and KAI rules/structure lens), strengths/weaknesses (team type lens and KAI subscores), communications (functions and originality lens), and creative problem solving/decision making (dynamics and KAI lens). In the end, we shifted four people on the subteams and reframed a number of the project management responsibility areas and relationships.

Level 1: (Effectiveness), 2: (Efficiency), and 3: (Improving)

From that point on, the KAI and MBTI learnings became major leverage points for the teams. The depth of personal insights into self and others was really amazing. We were able to use the group's KAI knowledge and understanding to re-form and rebalance the five actual work teams, which were later formed according to specific areas of focus and to regularly defuse stress and tension points around proposed ideas, process changes, and implementation planning. Again, this tool significantly accelerated the team's ability to work together and get things done.

The End Results (Level 7—Impossible)

Fifty-five percent in savings for the entire FWP manufacturing operation will accrue out of the Re-creation Thinking Expedition—an estimated $25 million (New Zealand dollars) through a wide range of changes at all levels:

55% savings!

Level 1

Formation of commodity teams to focus on key improvement areas for procurement sourcing strategies (e.g., going from managing engineering spares inventory, which was labor, time, and inventory intensive, to outsourcing to a local MRO parts supplier to manage the process).

152

Level 2

FWP changed focus to total systems costs versus the best price for purchasing.

Level 2

Owens Freight Company took over the process of managing domestic freight through focus on reducing overall costs versus competitively bidding for services.

Level 3

Improved communications between sales (demand) and manufacturing (supply) in order to lower inventory levels.

Level 3

Enhanced meeting processes, appropriate tools, and training resulted in dramatic percentage reduction in inventory.

Level 4

Rationalized products of marginal profitability and non-strategic long-term fit.

Level 5

Benchmarked other companies outside the wood products industry for an understanding of how to improve processes through best product tours worldwide. Key staff actually went to see how people were doing things better in other industries. (Example: Toyota New Zealand's inventory systems to keep finished goods and raw materials inventories to a minimum through the use of a pull versus a push system to service customers.)

Level 6

Targeting to design quality systems that break industry paradigms on scrap and waste in manufacturing hardboard and coated hardboard product.

Level 6

Switching scheduling from more than 50 percent Make-to-Stock to more than 80 percent Made-to-Orders.

Level 6

Defining a clear and distinct value proposition for the marketplace to drive the type of processes and systems and shaping the organization to enable employees to make the tough decisions.

To Copy . . .

MindShift

Copy Things

"See" and Notice

Level 7
Combining into one project the Thinking Expedition's philosophy and team dynamics, reengineering approach, and turnaround techniques.
Level 7
Relocating FWP head office from Greenlane to the Penrose manufacturing facility to lower costs during a major turnaround time frame with maximum change to manage.

CAMPBELL JUNIOR HIGH SCHOOL, CYPRESS-FAIRBANKS INDEPENDENT SCHOOL DISTRICT, HOUSTON, TEXAS

The Expedition School !

How do you energize junior high school teachers and students? Gwen Keith, the principal of Campbell Junior High School in the Cypress-Fairbanks Independent School District of Houston, Texas, did it by running her school like a Thinking Expedition on a day-to-day basis. She had attended the School for Innovators (Expedition XIV—April 1995) on a scholarship and had been immediately taken with the power of the expedition concept and the tools and techniques used to teach creative thinking. At the time, she was principal of Frazier Elementary School, but shortly after she returned, and before she could try out many of the new ideas she had, Gwen was promoted laterally to become the principal of a junior high school.

New to junior high and moving into a new leadership position, Gwen found her different (Level 6) ideas met with some resistance. To further complicate her ideas, she wanted her new school to be run by teams. Initially, in August 1995, her teachers and staff voted it down. But Gwen didn't quit. One year later, only five eighth-grade teachers were not on teams.

How? By ootching in change.

Levels 1 and 2: (Changes)
On the first day of her Thinking Expedition, Gwen introduced the idea of Blue Slips and asked plenty of tough questions. The next morning she began her work on team

154

Team Dynamics;
Learning Differences

building. At 2:00 P.M., she taught the entire staff how to tie a water knot, a basic mountaineering tool for securing webbing and ropes. She had learned how to tie the knot during the School for Innovators while rock climbing. She then formed them all up into small rope teams.

Level 1: (Change)

Her first goal was to form the A Team (Administration) into a working team. The A Team consists of a principal, director of instruction, assistant principals, counselors, and diagnostician. My partner, Dale Clauson, conducted a half-day KAI and MBTI workshop for the A Team, which then led to their supporting using another staff development day to have Dale come back and train the entire school of 125 professionals and paraprofessionals on KAI and MBTI (a Level 5 change and a good example of ootching).

To emphasize the expedition theme, Gwen says she used the theme of risk taking and teamwork throughout all of her staff development activities. While most of the actual changes she initially implemented at Campbell were lower-level changes, the idea of running the school like a Thinking Expedition was beyond Level 7 (Impossible) for many of the teachers and administrators. But, in August, at the start of the 1996 school year, I went out and, with Gwen helping as a guide, launched a volunteer team of fourteen sixth-, seventh-, and eighth-grade teachers as a Thinking Expedition at Campbell. They would in turn be leading 360 of the 1,100 students on a special Expedition Track for the next ten months.

Gwen's still going. Her school is always on expedition looking for ways to keep Campbell on the innovation track.

Following are some excerpts from Gwen's Thinking Expedition Journal notes outlining some of the changes realized.

Level 1: (Effectiveness)

"We worked on team building with the A Team. Established new ways of doing business with them. Approached the mountain very slowly. Decided what I would ignore and what I would change regarding past practices of how the

THINKING ABOUT THINKING

Level 5 Change
Seeing Things

A Team meetings worked. Did a lot of talk regarding expeditions and risk taking."

Level 2: (Efficiency)
"Sent Laurence Binder, director of instruction, to the School for Innovators in September 1995 (Expedition XV), so we could speak the same language and hook into the mission together. Later sent Assistant Principal Bonnie Pnegra to a School for Innovators sponsored by Exxon Chemicals (Expedition XVII) just for educators. Built off of the expertise of other members of the A Team."

Level 5: (Copying)
"Had Dale Clauson do a half-day workshop on MBTI and KAI. Began to get results and buy into the Thinking Expedition idea and teaming. The A Team decided that the entire staff should do MBTI and KAI!"

Level 3: (Improving), Level 6: (Different), and Level 4: (Cutting)
"Converted a storeroom into Base Camp. Used the expedition theme for decorations. Have mountain–climbing artwork on walls. Large table to work together (Level 3). Began to hold A Team meetings here for problem solving, setting goals. There was a sense of change in the air as we worked in the room together very differently than we had elsewhere before (Level 6). No phone in the Base Camp conference room (Level 4). We are on expedition, therefore no interruptions from outside."

Level 5: (Copying) and Level 6: (Different)
"We copied ourselves! I used the A Team and what it had learned to change the format of the faculty meetings (Level 6). They had been done the same way since 1978 right down to people sitting in the same chairs. We used Blue Slips (Level 1, but for this group Level 6!). We modeled teaming by using the A Team as an example (Level 5). We walked our talk. We conducted the meeting as a team. Got people up out of their chairs

Gwen's tip! "On a journey into change, don't forget to stop, look back over your shoulder... see how far you've come."

156

and moving around. A Team members became facilitators for meetings and taught tools like Brain Writing and Blue Slips."

The Results (Level 5)

Gwen's ideas and example are spilling over (Level 5)into other schools in Cypress–Fairbanks Independent School District, and CyFair ISD now has a large cadre of educators who are graduates of the School for Innovators. Special assessment and measurement processes are being developed to monitor (Level 2) the long-term effects and changes of the Expedition track on student learning. Whatever they are, excitement and enthusiasm is high for students and teachers alike!

R. J. REYNOLDS R&D INNOVATION WEEK, CHARLOTTESVILLE, VIRGINIA

The leadership team of R. J. Reynolds Bowman Grey Research Center approached us in late 1992, to help them design and roll out an innovation initiative. "We don't want to do this the way we did Quality," was the going-in position (i.e., "We don't want a Level 5 approach"). Quality had been a long, careful, top-down, gradual but steady rollout resulting in dissipated energy across the R&D Center. "We want innovation to start at the end with the kickoff, and we want to train all eight hundred people at one time."

What a mandate. Our immediate reaction was Impossible! Can't be done! No way! You'd have to rent the coliseum downtown to pull that off, just for starters. Excited, the steering group said, "Wow! What a great idea! You guys really do think different."

So we hit on the approach of J.I.T. everything. Our underlying concept was first to run a very focused School for Innovators to train and arm a cadre of thirty-four innovation facilitators. They would then work in pairs, teaching classes of twenty to twenty-four people at a time, and we would lineback them during the rollout. The Innovation Steering Group researched and compiled a tool kit filled with a wide variety of innovation and creativity tools, techniques, technologies, processes, and reference materials, and worked with us to develop a

"A great thought begins by seeing something differently, with a shift of the minds eye."

· *Albert Einstein*

skeleton outline for a one-day, eight-hour class on innovation, which the pairs of facilitators would flesh out and teach. We then scheduled and ran the five-day School for Innovators built around the basic Creative Problem Solving (CPS) model, thinking different, hands-on practice in a wide range of techniques for small group leadership and some Me, Inc.®

We also rented the coliseum.

During the mini-school, the facilitator pairs began designing their own eight-hour innovation class, resulting in seventeen very different (Level 5 and 6 changes) approaches and agendas. (This was a clear Level 7 change for us—there was no way it was going to work!) The week following the mini-school, all the facilitators polished and practiced. The week after that, we returned to launch Innovation Week and coach them as it unfolded over four days. Each pair of innovators taught twenty-four people a day. By Friday morning, everyone had been baptized in a wide range of innovation philosophies, and we were ready for the BIG BANG—the kickoff at the end of the rollout instead of at the beginning.

The coliseum was packed with the gang of eight hundred. The facilitator pairs were distributed through the assembly, and the lights went out. The "voice of the skeptic" quietly broadcast over loudspeakers out into the darkness, wondering what this was all about, how it could possibly be of value, why they were all here, and on and on and on. Then, BAM! The lights went up, and the executive vice president of R&D, Carl Ehmann, and I took the group through the 7 Levels of Change around which were wrapped both corporate and personal Me, Inc.® thinking. The morning focused on (idea-finding) mindshifts, mission, vision, values, and personal strategies for innovation. It was absolutely dynamite! People went out the door with their hair on fire.

17 Different Innovation Classes!

The Results (short term: Level 7)

After Innovation Week, the momentum continued. R&D set up a series of four "Mindshift Fridays," which started immediately. In these sessions, supervisory personnel and a facilitator

158

pair met with work groups to discuss how they would capture and act on new ideas (Level 1 and Level 6). The second follow-up was the replacement of the Innovation Steering Committee with a new leadership group called "The 7th Level" to work to define a new mission for innovation in R&D using ideas from employees (a definite Level 7).

The Results (long term: Level 7)

In February of 1995, R. J. Reynolds was honored as the first recipient of the George Land World Class Innovator award at the annual Innovative Thinking Network Convergence in Santa Barbara, California. R. J. Reynolds was chosen primarily for taking a leadership role in building a culture that promotes risk taking through the interactive combination of teamwork, innovation, and diversity. R. J. Reynolds made innovation a goal, and, in the three years since innovation week, dramatically changed the corporate culture at R. J. Reynolds R&D. Although the company has not reached the number one position in its industry, its ability to adapt rapidly has improved tremendously, and R. J. Reynolds R&D has made innovative inroads into such diverse areas as the worldwide fragrance industry, niche marketing, emission monitoring, and new international product introductions.

CADILLAC FAIRVIEW, TORONTO, CANADA

Cadillac Fairview, a major Canadian real estate company with head offices in Toronto, had undergone four years of restructuring, downsizing, and major financial challenges. During that time, the company took a hiatus from its traditional national conference. Then, in June of 1996, the conference was brought back with the theme of "Taking charge—*Foncer!*"

Mary Jane Grant, a real innovator and management consultant I had met at the 41st Creative Problem Solving Institute in Buffalo, introduced me over the phone to Scott Knaut, a professional conference organizer, and then connected me with Peter Sharpe, Cadillac Fairview's executive vice president for operations. Peter was putting together the

Taking charge of Change!

FOCUS on CHANGE

design of the National Conference to set the stage for pushing down responsibility into the organization to give employees ownership in the business. Along with this initiative came a new vision, mission, and set of values. Peter is a real adventurer and had been on safari in Kenya the previous year. We clicked, and the Thinking Expedition format was on.

Then, BAM! everything shifted to a very high level of change for us. Planning and executing this Thinking Expedition was not going to start with an easy ootching process from Level 1.

A Level 7 Start

The first big challenge was that this would be a ninety-person Thinking Expedition. While we had led thirty-six-person expeditions before and had the experience of R. J. Reynolds' BIG BANG Innovation Week with eight hundred-plus participants, we had never run a large-party Thinking Expedition in intense format (14-hour days!). I went back to Houston and thought about it. We came up with what we thought would be an exciting flow built around Me, Inc.®

I called Mary Jane and discovered to my horror that the group's size had grown to 120. We went back and rethought the design. Cadillac Fairview went back and rethought the size. In two more conversations the expedition topped out at 170, nearly a 100 percent increase over the original concept (Level 7 Change). This isn't a problem with a conference, but a Thinking Expedition is anything but a meeting or a training session. We rethought some more (thanks to R. J. Reynolds, this was now "only" a Level 6 challenge for us).

More Level 7 Change

Somewhere along the team size growth curve, we also transitioned into having the group not only focus on personal exploration and growth (the original idea) but also to have the 170-person team somehow come up with a new Cadillac Fairview vision, mission, and set of values. While an operating vision and mission and an inventory of team values and strengths are part and parcel of every Thinking

160

170+ person Thinking Expedition

The Focus: New vision, mission, values

Expedition, the degree of interaction and exercises we would need to drive them out had just exploded beyond our wildest comprehension with the growth to nearly two hundred people.

Level 6

Finally, Cadillac Fairview had just launched a companywide reengineering project and wanted to include a meaningful update on its status during the National Conference. We mindshifted into high gear. First, we had to realign management expectations away from "National Conference" to "Thinking Expedition." Second, I had to sell a "no agenda" agenda (trust the Expedition Guide with the route and process). And third, we had to integrate everything and make it all work!

Levels 5 and 4

We gradually seemed to be backing down into more manageable levels of change and started redesigning again based on successful experiences with some of our other Thinking Expeditions. Because of the 170-person size, our design work was primarily focused on what to cut out of our normal expedition route plan.

Using Level 4 to Solve Level 6 and 7 Challenges

Most of the big challenges for us were tied up in the size of the team, preprocessing volume, and time. We decided to cut out the Myers-Briggs Inventory (MBTI) and use only the Kirton Adaption-Innovation (KAI) Inventory (Levels 4 and 2). Still, getting 170 KAI forms and each person's Expedition VISA (a one-page, pre-expedition questionnaire) mailed to us prior to the Expedition in time for us to process and analyze the information became a real Level 7 job. We discovered that growth in team size in large numbers was not a straight line progression in terms of difficulty for us—it was a rapidly increasing upward curve, much like the one we use to describe the shifts between each level of change.

THINKING ABOUT THINKING

Adaptive Thinking
· Copy
- Notice more
- Stop and stare
- Clip newspapers and magazines
- Combine and synthesize
- LEVEL 5 THINKING

The group size was going to pack the large (now small!) banquet building in which we would be holding the Thinking Expedition, even with eight people to a small rope team (twenty-one tables).

Levels 1, 2, and 6
On Day One, the launch at Orillia, Ontario (two hours north of Toronto) was both very focused and very different. We began (imprinting) the expedition the minute people stepped out of their cars or off the buses from the airport (a ninety-minute trip). We formed up a base camp team, which issued equipment and gear on the spot: BAM!—vests, hats, Thinking Expedition passports, the VISA process, Thinking Journals, Blue Slips, room reservations, and team assignments. We got everyone into execution and doing something immediately to create a heightened sense of urgency. This was different!

Tip! Immediately imprint "Diffferent" continued to build on Diffferent...

Level 6
We kicked off the Thinking Expedition with a very brief, "noninformative" welcome by Peter Sharpe to deliberately keep the unknown unclear and moved full-bore into doing things different. Video clips, 35mm slides, music, and a constant shifting of the makeup of the twenty-one eight-person teams were the catalysts for the first evening.

Levels 1, 2, 3, 4, 5, and 6
On Day Two, we moved slowly into the unknown, thinking about thinking, thinking before we thought, and exploring personal strengths, values, and beliefs as well as issues, challenges, and opportunities. Thinking Journals were used extensively, and by nightfall, everyone was comfortable with the Levels 1, 2, and 3 changes in both their doing and thinking that had taken place over the day. They were now competent in basic creative thinking and idea-finding tools and techniques, had gotten to know a large number of new people quickly and much more deeply than expected, had made significant mindshifts, and were beginning to be ready for anything. Following the guides' lead (Level 5), they had

162

begun to drop old thinking habits and patterns (Level 4), and we made rapid progress on the long trek in. And at dinnertime on Day Two, to improve the team dynamics, we went to six-person teams (Level 4), increasing to twenty-eight tables and absolutely jamming the room. The learning, however, was that when people returned from dinner to find everything different, their sense of intensity and urgency immediately increased. Late on Day Two, the guides declared that we had reached "advanced base camp," and the rope teams settled down to reflect on where they were.

Levels 3, 4, 5, and 6

On Day Three the rope teams were re-formed and began to assess the mess—the mountain range of issues, challenges, and opportunities in front of them. Working now in regional groupings based on creative style (KAI scores), they began to explore common values and strengths and compared their personal missions and visions to reach some initial consensus on what the new Cadillac Fairview could become. Building on these insights, they cut through the extraneous data rapidly (Level 4), coming up with new and different ideas and thinking (Level 6) to sketch out potential locations for higher camps and routes for a summit attempt (missions and visions). Once their thinking and mountains had more clarity, the teams sent scouts out to learn from the explorations and discoveries of other teams (Level 5). Note: During the mountain building work, the teams were organized homogeneously by KAI scores. (i.e., everyone on a team had closely similar scores).

Level 6

Assault on the summit of Mt. Cadillac Fairview! Late on Day Three, with temperature readings among the teams reaching amazing levels (this is a quick-check process we use in which everyone writes down their "temperature"—their mental/energy level—on a scale of zero to ten, then discusses it as a table team, averages it, and calls it out to the rest of the group), the teams began work on the breakout and

Watch

QUESTION:

What Trends Should We Be Watching?

...BLUE SLIP

breakthrough ideas and thinking that had the potential to put them on the summit of the mountains they had created.

Level 6
High Camp. Agreement on the vision, mission, and values of the new Cadillac Fairview came together with a fluidity and excitement that was overpowering. Balance, respect, integrity, communications, knowledge, and smiles were very clearly the underlying and guiding values that connected with everyone—coupled with a vision of being the best and most dynamic real estate organization in the world.

Level 7
By the evening of Day Three, eight of the teams had put breakout and breakthrough ideas on the summit (ideas on how to roll out and implement the new vision/mission and values), and a large number of other BIG Ideas (Levels 4, 5, and 6 thinking) were produced as well. The entire expedition started the descent back to base camp and prepared for the long trek home.

Levels 1 and 2
On the morning of Day Four, the teams gathered to start the process of turning their discoveries and BIG Ideas into results and action plans. The focus was on thinking effectively and efficiently about how to implement them and how to creatively roll out and engage everyone else in the new Cadillac Fairview vision, mission, and values. The teams were leveraging the momentum and energy created by the Thinking Expedition. We also debriefed them on their KAI scores and how they had played out during the Expedition.

Levels 1, 2, 3, 5, and 6
Two months later, the leadership group at each Cadillac Fairview property (all of whom had been on the Thinking Expedition at Orillia) engaged employees at their location on lines similar (Level 5) to what they

The values, mission & vision...

Strategies for the New Cadillac Fairview

164

themselves had experienced. Creative thinking and innovation tools and techniques were used to bring out personal beliefs, values, goals, and ideas. These were then synthesized into the vision, mission, and values for their particular property using Blue Slips, Five-Minute Meetings, BIG Ideas (Levels 1, 2, and 3), and the 7 Levels of Change. After that was finished, the company's vision, mission, and values were revealed (Level 6), and work was begun to tie the employees' individual thinking into the company's statements.

Level 6

Looking back at where we've been, a very new and different Cadillac Fairview was created by the people who make the company what it is. They are "Taking Charge—*Foncer!*"

U.S. NAVY SMART SHIP PROJECT, USS YORKTOWN

The SMART SHIP Project was launched by Admiral Mike Boorda, chief of naval operations, in November of 1995. Admiral Boorda laid out his vision clearly in a message to the fleet. Commissioning the SMART SHIP Project, he said that the navy was faced with challenging fiscal choices. "It is imperative that we keep fleet performance high while striving to operate our ships more efficiently," Admiral Boorda said. "Personnel expenses combine to utilize over one-half of the navy budget, and I am initiating a project called 'SMART SHIP' which will help us focus on ways to achieve the benefits of reduced ship crew size."

Admiral Boorda set the focus clearly: "Today, we can explore improvements through the application of proven, currently available technology, changes in shipboard equipment, embedded training, and a new look at shipboard personnel requirements." To emphasize the importance of making something happen fast, Admiral Boorda designated the USS YORKTOWN, a large guided missile cruiser with a crew of 370, as the operational platform on which to test ideas.

Action Plans

THINKING ABOUT THINKING
Adaptive Thinking
· **Steal good thinking**
- **Learn from others**
- **Model great thinkers**
- **Copy others thinking processes**
- **Collect unusual questions**

- LEVEL 5 THINKING

The Level 7 mindshifter, however, and the words that really opened things up were: ". . . we must be willing to selectively break with culture and tradition and employ technology as a work saver—not as backup."

And with that, the SMART SHIP Team got under way.

Captain Tom Zysk was named the project team leader. At the kickoff meeting on November 15, 1995, the team started by describing the SMART SHIP Program as "a rare opportunity to revolutionize. Technology is not a roadblock—manning can be reduced substantially using only demonstrated technology. The roadblocks are to be found in culture and tradition."

The navy's approach centered on setting up a single operational ship to serve as a model using innovative technology aimed at reducing manning requirements and life-cycle costs. The SMART SHIP Project goal was to install and maintain (through the demonstration period) innovative projects onboard a U.S. Navy commissioned surface ship and demonstrate the resulting reductions in manpower and benefits associated with life-cycle costs.

The navy was committed to working outside the box on this project and was willing to accept any and all ideas for evaluation—in all areas that might be a candidate for reducing manpower requirements onboard surface ships as long as they would not have an adverse impact on readiness or create additional manpower demands on other requirements such as operations, training, logistics supportability, maintainability, and reliability.

Captain Tom Zysk called me almost immediately after the team was formed and asked if we could put together a short course on out-of-the-box thinking, and innovation tools and techniques for the team of twenty naval officers and civilian engineers. We agreed on the format of a two-stage "lite" Thinking Expedition, which would heavily emphasize applying creativity tools and techniques on first-cut idea finding for the SMART SHIP. Chief Petty Officer David Purkiss, a graduate of our July 1994 School for Innovators, clipped in to assist me as an Expedition Guide.

". . . selectively break with culture and tradition . . ." U.S. NAVY??

166

Another "ENT" CHANGE TEAM!

Potential BIG Hole!

SMART SHIP *Team Profile*

Although we were going in on short notice, the team completed the KAI and MBTI and overnighted them back to us. Prior to that I had made an operating/planning assumption that the group's profile would be that of traditional military officers: TJ, conservative, and biased toward the adaptive side of the KAI scale. Further, I thought that they would generally have an engineering mind-set/background. Well, in the end, they didn't. They were delightfully different, diverse, unnormal, a lot of fun to work with, and full of new thinking.

Their responses with MBTI showed them to be a pretty solid ENTJ team, and they had a strong innovator average KAI score 4-Sigma off the norm. The typical ENTJ team intuitively grasps change, takes command, and acts decisively. They are focused outward and respond quickly to external shifts, developments, and opportunities. Looking for possibilities, they have no difficulty coming up with big and visionary changes as well as strategies for implementing them. They plan well and handle any and all of the 7 Levels of Change easily.

Often an ENTJ team will have a tendency to approach things with an "engineering" mind-set—an impersonal point of view of the issues and factors connected with the problem—and because of that, they are not particularly well suited for major changes centered around people. The team had almost no Feeling types at all, a huge hole in understanding people. This flagged a concern for both Chief Petty Officer Purkiss and me—the whole thrust of the SMART SHIP Project was built on sailors, and sailors would have to implement the changes in the end.

ENTJ teams can grow quite large and still remain focused and effective. They hate inefficiency and don't tolerate incompetence. They like things spelled out and definite. They focus on closure, and they aim for clear results.

With a KAI average score strongly biased towards the innovative side, they were well suited for their out-of-the-box thinking mission. A team with scores such as they had can easily be perceived as fitting with the normal organization, can slip in innovations under that appearance, and is usually good at manipulating adaptive structures. Their high originality score would ensure out-of-the-box concepts, and there was a high probability that their innovative ideas would have practical applications and could be implemented easily. They would be intuitive in their approaches and very comfortable determining their own agenda.

Starting with their ENTJ type in mind, we pushed them into 2-Sigma thinking quickly, running a pretty focused "lite" expedition. We worked primarily at setting the stage for thinking different—Think 101 basics—and for recognizing that this was in fact a Thinking Expedition into the unknown. We concentrated on arming the team with creative thinking tools and skills for changing at Levels 1 through 6 :

This was our "going in" assessment...

Level 1 Change
How to have an idea with Blue Slips: "Write it down!"

Level 1 Change
How to interact with other people and capture their thinking and ideas.

Level 1 Change
Developing the ability to play with ideas.

Level 2 Change
What to do with their ideas once they had some; how to process their thinking.

Level 3 Change
How to leverage each other, particularly the diversity of thinking styles within the team; the power of two—Pairing-and-Sharing ideas and concepts.

Level 4 Change
Suspending judgment as long as possible, focusing on positive thinking/perspectives first before moving into negative or critical thinking.

168

Level 4 Change
How to change the nature of meetings and briefings into creative, innovative idea-finding sessions.

Level 5 Change
Noticing, clipping, and copying ideas, shifts, and trends in magazines, newspapers, journals, movies, and TV.

Level 5 Change
We taught the team the Creative Education Foundation's (CEF) basic Creative Problem Solving (CPS) model and how to apply each stage of the model depending on the challenge or problem. I also explained the rules/roles (Level 2 Change) of brainstorming and modeled how to apply those within CPS. Then I coached Captain Ross Barker, one of the senior team members, through stand-up use of the CPS process (thirty-minute version) with the team on a real SMART SHIP focus area problem. With Ross, we had imprinted Level 6, different—a navy captain leading a CPS session! He set the tone and the team was off and running.

Level 6 Change
We had the team work on several different things grouped by their KAI/MBTI scores (as usual, without their knowing it). Afterward, I explained KAI and MBTI theory, gave the team individual and group feedback on their scores, and pointed out where differences were clearly operating among them. We worked through understanding how each member of the team individually approached problem solving, idea finding, and action finding/solution finding. The team learned how to leverage differences and diversity in the group. I focused on helping the team understand the differences in creative style within the group—and how to flex and cope with those differences to maximize the diversity as much as possible.

Level 4, 5, 6, and 7 Changes
We worked through a number of BIG Idea exercises focused on coming up with out-of-the-box concepts and departed with the team wired up and ready to go make things happen.

LEVEL 5
Copying

Technology Transfer

...CONTINUOUS INNOVATION

Level 6 change: Captain Tom Zysk called me again almost as soon as I got back to Houston. He was excited about the results we'd gotten with the mini-expedition and the noticeable shifts in thinking and energy the team had picked up. Tom wanted to know if we could come back for a second stage the next week to both form up the team a bit tighter and leverage the momentum we had created. Chief Purkiss and I turned around and went back the week before Christmas and the team easily moved to higher levels of thinking and doing with more tools and techniques. They were more than ready for change and really connected to thinking differently.

Looking back, this was one of the most exciting and rewarding things I've ever been involved with—a great project, absolutely superb, innovative, motivated people, and a lot of them officers in the U.S. Navy! For me, personally, it was a real Level 7 mindshift—it couldn't be happening. (As an air force colonel with twenty-five years on active duty, I knew what I knew!)

Consider that the project was started without program funding with the intention of seeking funding for all projects found to be advantageous to the navy. And more Level 6: In addition to traditional contracting methods, all types of acquisition and nonacquisition methods were to be utilized, including cooperative agreements and other collaborative efforts between the government and industry. Any kind of transaction was to be used when other forms of procurement weren't feasible.

Level 7 Change

Instead of issuing a formal Request for Proposal (RFP), as is the normal approach under the Federal Acquisition Regulations (FAR), the SMART SHIP Team issued a Broad Agency Announcement (BAA). The BAA allowed the SMART SHIP Team to express its intention and interests and to solicit any and all ideas without implying that anything further would happen with the ideas. Further, the BAA had no telephone numbers in it—rather, it directed interested parties to access an Internet server on the World Wide Web to submit proposals or to ask questions. Some five hundred-plus proposals were received in the first five months, and the contracting office only had to mail out five information packages. A project of this scope normally would have generated requests for literally thousands of information packages. Of course, this wasn't a normal navy project! Proposals were submitted by E-mail with attached disks (Level 6 change) and were limited to ten pages in length.

Electronic Commerce!

Level 4 Change

This allowed the project officers on the team to get some work done instead of answering the phone all the time and reading proposals for the first six months. It generated an E-mail explosion. Any callers who did manage to get through were told, "Go read the Web page."

There was some resistance to taking this approach (Level 7 change) with the Broad Agency Announcement. Critics shrieked that it couldn't be done, that the Q&A section could not be built into the Web page. In the end it worked great. Everyone submitting a proposal had access to the same information and answers. More than eight hundred concepts and proposals were ultimately received.

The team worked hard through the spring and early summer of '96, and, predictably, got pretty focused. They wrote up the ideas as one-page SMART SHIP Implementation Proposals (SSIPs) and then implemented and bolted as many as they could onto the ship. This phase was primarily idea finding, idea processing, and relatively small-scale implementations of lower level changes. Any ideas requiring large-scale physical changes and major engineering work were queued into the future.

By June of 1996, the SMART SHIP Team had been nominated for The Hammer Award for reinventing government, and it looked like the life of the team was going to be extended.

TEAM II—SECOND PHASE, JUNE 1996

Captain Tom Zysk called me again and asked me to do some planning on how to transition in a new team to replace most of the old one. He would be retiring in June, and most of the team members would go back to their primary commands

Copy

What could we

Copy? ...BLUE SLIP

since they had only been on loan to the SMART SHIP Project. With replacements coming in, Captain Grey Glover had been named to lead the project into the next phase of implementation and measurement. Tom felt Team II would need to go through everything the first team had and thought that a one-shot (instead of two-stage) Thinking Expedition would be the way to go.

Commander Bill Olsen, a real out-of-the-box innovator on the first team, began the planning with me, and Chief Petty Officer David Purkiss and I went back to Carderock Naval Warfare Center in early August for a three-day Thinking Expedition.

The mission and objectives were team building/bonding and innovation tools and techniques. Then, BAM! just before we left, we learned that Vice Admiral D. J. Katz, the executive director for the SMART SHIP Project, was going to show up in the middle of Day Three of the Thinking Expedition for a briefing on the project. Several other unexpected events combined to make this look more and more like an operational expedition:

SMART SHIP Thinking Expedition II

Level 1 Change
Because of the rotation of 85 percent of the original SMART SHIP Project team in June, we had designed a fast-forward, two-day-plus (42 hours!) Thinking Expedition focused on bringing them up to speed on innovation tools, techniques, and thinking different. We also developed some ideas for assessment of implemented ideas on the SMART SHIP, and in the process built a new team.

1300 ≠ 3:00pm . . .

We showed up ninety minutes late for our kickoff with the new team. Our plan was to come in at 3:00 P.M., but their plan had been to start with us at 1300 hours. This was a great way to start—doing the right things; NOT!

Level 2 Change
After giving up on our arrival, the team had moved into developing an update briefing for Vice Admiral Katz —doing the right things right.

172

The 5-Minute meeting works!

Level 3 Change

Coming in late as we had, we walked into the middle of the discussion on the briefing design. Chief Purkiss immediately stepped into the breach and kick-started the group with a Five-Minute Meeting—a simple Level 3 change for us. For the team, however, it was pure Level 6 different! The energy level of the room went right through the roof. David had them Pair-And-Share the ideas they had just written down (a Level 2 change).

> NOTE: This was the only time we demonstrated and taught the how-tos of the Five-Minute Meeting. Keep your eye on LCDR Ed Kenyon as this expedition unfolds. Ed is a strong adaptor with an amazing innovative streak.

Level 1 Change

When the team settled back down, we started at Level 1 and did the right thing. We moved into a quick overview of what a Thinking Expedition is, how we were going to operate and lead it (rules and roles), and how an expedition works. This was not our normal, no-agenda-up-front approach. However, we've learned over time that for a team with a strong STJ bias, up-front clarity and details are pretty important. We had sent the new team KAI and MBTI inventories to complete prior to our arrival and already knew what to expect.

Level 6 Change

Different and unexpected: We discovered that Captain Jim Baskerville, commander of the Carderock R&D Center and cochairman of the steering group for the team, had decided to join the Thinking Expedition. My own air force mental filters put navy captains at the far end of conservative. Here I was with three of them! Jim gave me a fast mindshift. He proved to be a real innovator, open to anything, and ready to make just about anything happen.

Level 2 Change

Straight off, we introduced the team to the process of capturing ideas by writing them down on Blue Slips and Just In

---

Level 6 Thinking
Change HOW You Think

· **Think about the way you think**
· **Shift your perceptions**
· **Look at things differently**
· **Follow your intuition**
· **Force connections**
· **Be different**
     ...lateral thinking

Time (J.I.T.) journaling. Only four people remained from the original team, so this was essentially all new stuff for the team. They'd been hearing about Blue Slips and idea capturing, seen others using them, but weren't quite sure about them yet.

Level 4 Change

Chief Purkiss got the team to write their expectations for the Expedition on Blue Slips. Then he had them wad them up and throw them away, a straightforward Level 4 change (cutting out blocks to new thinking). We moved from that on into negative self-talk and both team and external Not Invented Here (NIH).

Then Vice Admiral Katz's perturbation began to register on the expedition. He was going to be coming in the next day, and Captain Grey Glover and the newbies on the team were starting to defocus. Grey was open, though, and we decided to use the briefing as a mission objective for the Thinking Expedition. We used the tools and techniques the team was learning to explore and get ready for the briefing. From here we mindshifted into higher levels of thinking fast.

Tip! Get rid of expectations fast!

Level 6 Changes and more

We taught the team Mindmapping and a lateral thinking crayon technique we call Picasso. Forming them into small rope teams by KAI scores, each team had to imagine (Level 7) that they were the only ones who were going to brief the admiral and that they had to use their Mindmaps to do it. Further, that it had to be Level 6 different because by this time, they realized that was what the SMART SHIP was about.

Mindmapping the Admiral's briefing

Level 7

Grey Glover stood up on his chair exactly like Robin Williams in *The Dead Poets Society* and told the team that he was going to start off the briefing with Admiral Katz that way. He intended to give him a very minimal outline of what was going to be covered, no timeline for when it would be over, and let the team run with it. A lot of mouths dropped open in the room—this was a real Mindshift. Nobody believed him, but . . . crayons and mindmaps started flying, and it was difficult to shut things down at 10:30 P.M. that night (2230 in navyspeak).

Level 6 and 7 Changes

The next morning we pressed on, now reorganizing the teams into their actual working areas relative to the project. Using the previous night's Crazy Ideas and diverse Mindmaps, they focused in and created five major Mindmaps to cover every aspect of the status in each functional area. The energy level on the expedition had gone through the roof again. We then loaded up and drove from the offsite location back to Carderock and the SMART SHIP Team base camp to set up for Vice Admiral Katz.

Level 7 Change

The summit: Grey Glover was unreal. When he said "Admiral" and climbed up on his chair, the team was galvanized. He did exactly what he said he'd do! The Mindmaps seemed like second nature, and Admiral Katz played right into them as each team walked him through them. At the end, just as Grey Glover was about to close the briefing, Lieutenant Commander Ed Kenyon stood up and said to Captain Glover, "Just a minute, sir. Admiral Katz, we're going to run a Hot Wash-up Five-Minute Meeting. If I could ask you and everyone else to take some of these Blue Slips—" and quiet Ed, with the strongest adaptive KAI score on the team, ran a perfectly executed Five-Minute Meeting. He then paired up Admiral Katz and Grey Glover to share their Blue Slip ideas, along with the whole team. The place was electrified! It was magic.

The Payoff?

From my vantage point—$500 million to $1 billion in long-term savings. Where'd that figure come from? The YORK-TOWN was commissioned July 4, 1984. She's twelve years old and has an expected ship life of thirty-five

The Return of the 5-Minute Meeting

Diffferent

dif·fer·ent (dĂf"ör-önt, dĂf"rönt) Adj. 1, Unlike in form, quantity, or amount or, nature; Dissimilar: 2. Distinct, or separate: 3. Differing from all others; distinct.

years, leaving twenty-two years of remaining ship life. Using a cost figure of $34,000 per year per manpower slot times the ship life, with a projected reduction of fifty billets or military positions, YORKTOWN could save the navy $37 million. One hundred billets, the high-end estimate, would yield $75 million in savings. Carrying this out into the fleet in YORKTOWN's class of ship only, with forty-seven ships in the class, overall long-term savings would be $500 million to $1 billion.

The Results

A few of the many changes implemented on the SMART SHIP in the first six months:

Level 1 Change

Shifted all hands to coveralls, making laundry simpler and faster.

Reduced Fire Watch requirements. SMART SHIP Team hit upon a change to the traditional way of manning fire watches, which had been an exhaustive workload on the crew. This change was immediately passed on to the fleet. This was a leap of faith in the face of policy and has potential to reduce occasional fire watch requirements both at sea and in port by 50 percent.

Level 2

New Automated Tag Out System (ATOS) called Taglink replaced a cumbersome, manual safety program. Taglink is a proven Dbase III Windows–based software program that performs the ATOS functions with significantly reduced workload and a substantial increase in audit accuracy. Will realize a 50 to 60 percent reduction in all work centers using Taglink and will not eliminate billets but reduce collateral duties for four to five billets.

Level 2 Change

EZ Pup fire hose nozzle handling device. The process of breaking out, handling, maneuvering, and drilling/fighting

176

fires with the navy standard fire-fighting hose nozzles is tiring work. For that reason the navy trains and mans hose teams with sufficient numbers of people to rotate the No. 1 nozzle-man. The EZ Pup fire-hose nozzle-handling device can be readily backfitted onto any firehouse and significantly reduce effort, fatigue, and manpower associated with handling hoses. It allows the crew member on the front of the hose to run the hose for forty-five to sixty minutes without getting tired. Present equipment tires the front crew member in five minutes and requires continuous rotation of positions. The cost of the new nozzle is $300.

Level 5 Change

The change to Reliability Centered Maintenance (RCM) was a very dramatic change seen as quite risky, but private airlines have been doing it for quite some time. Much of the current preventative maintenance requirements are on a time-directed basis. RCM methodology emphasizes Condition-Based Maintenance, enabling direct workload savings by repairing only what needs to be repaired. It has an estimated bottom-line reduction of 30 percent of total maintenance man-hours shipwide.

Level 5 Change

Pilot house manning—take people off the bridge. The plan was to go from twelve people to a minimum manning of five as it is done in the Merchant Marine. Successful implementation resulted in a net reduction of twenty-one watch standers, 168 man hours per day, and required no funding, but does require watch standers to have more training.

Level 5 Change

Switched paintbrushes to Paint Sticks, a home use product from Home Products Corporation. Commander Bill Olsen, visiting the SMART SHIP, saw a Bosuns Mate painting a big bulkhead with a two-inch brush, dripping paint all over and getting paint on his uniform. Bill went home, got a Paint Stick, came back in uniform, and demonstrated how it worked without spilling a drop.

copy private airlines

copy the Merchant Marine!

and homeowners!

3 - Sigma Thinking

DIFFERENT

2%   2%

Level 6

Shifting to cashless services reduced operations for shipboard office, ship's store, vending machines, and Morale & Welfare expenses. The idea is tied to the use of a SmartCard as an enabling technology (doesn't reduce workload, improves quality of life). Saves one to three billets and reduces collateral duties for six to ten senior personnel.

Level 6

Instituted the use of the Smart ID Card called "MARC" for Multitechnology Automated Reader Card. MARC makes the process of properly and accurately identifying shipboard personnel significantly more efficient and accurate, reducing independently done and unintegrated administrative effort. Magnetic swipers/readers would be installed at all muster points and key watch locations, allowing accurate muster to be taken in minutes.

Level 7

The Broad Agency Announcement (BAA) process itself was an impossible idea that met incredible initial resistance. The attitude was "can't be done" because of the existing Federal Acquisition Regulations (FAR). The BAA allowed the SMART SHIP Team to express its intentions and interests only and to solicit any and all ideas without implying that anything further would happen with the ideas. Using the Web page saved time on both ends.

The Surprise

On August 29, 1996, the Honorable John Dalton, secretary of the navy, on behalf of Vice President Al Gore, presented the SMART SHIP Team with The Hammer Award for reinventing government processes in support of the President's National Performance Review Principles. The citation accompanying the award read:

"The navy's SMART SHIP is the antithesis of 'bureaucratic red tape.' The project brings together a very diverse group of energetic and talented civilian and military individuals representing a variety of organizations, who have succeeded in

www. SMART!
Electronic Commerce

178

breaking with past practices by challenging policy, culture, and tradition of procuring and operating navy ships. The SMART SHIP Team has been charged with rapidly changing policies and identifying new technologies which will reduce the workload for a navy ship's crew, improve sailors' quality of life, and enhance the ship's mission readiness."

The Aftermath
SMART SHIP Team members Commander Bill Olsen and Arnie Ostroff both attended the August 1996 School for Innovators in Estes Park, Colorado. Bill returned to find he'd been extended on the SMART SHIP Team, Stage II, and Arnie found himself on the new Smart Base Team. More navy Smart Expeditions are in the works.

Once you've hit the summit, Level 7 doesn't stay Level 7 for very long!

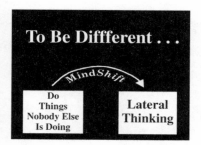

APPENDIX I

The process of mentally incorporating is an introspective exercise in personal change. Many people have never thought through who they are, who they have been, who they want to be or become, and what they are trying to do. Me, Inc.® is the process of mentally incorporating yourself as an intrapreneur or entrepreneur.

Me, Inc.® helps you develop a personal mission statement, take inventory of your values and strengths, determine your Critical Success Factors, come up with 101 personal goals, and create a vision of the future for yourself. It leads you through a structured process to create a "business plan" for life. Me, Inc.® was originally developed to reinforce the application of the curriculum of the School for Innovators.

Me, Inc.® is an entrepreneurial business built on your personal values, strengths, experiences, and ideas. As you mentally incorporate, you will discover your own power to focus your mission and strategy and learn how to continuously improve today and tomorrow as Me, Inc.® You will explore how you are unique and different and question assumptions you make about yourself.

Me, Inc.® builds on the process of thinking about thinking, your own unique ways of thinking, and your personal creative style. Me, Inc.® is a lengthy and deeply reflective process. As you can see from the following diagram, it is a progression through increasingly higher levels of change and mindshifts.

Me, Inc.
personal Thinking
Expedition

180

7 LEVELS OF PERSONAL CHANGE

Level of Change	Thinking about Thinking	Level of Thinking
1	Taking B+ inventory of basic qualities Skills, strengths, abilities	Focused Thinking
2	Amplifying strengths and skills Examining personal creative style and type Exploring personal operating principles Developing list of basic values and beliefs Exploring purpose (B-) Defining personal mission (B-)	J.I.T. Thinking
3	Beginning a list of 101 goals & wishes Examining risky experiences Reflecting on successes and mistakes Considering Critical Success Factors for Change Developing (B+) Strategy for Change (1-Sigma)	Positive Thinking
4	Expanding on 101 goals & wishes Examining traits, habits, biases, handicaps Expanding list of goals & wishes: Bad habits Re-exploring purpose Refining Strategy for Change (2-Sigma)	Reflective Thinking Refocused Thinking
5	Continue pushing forward with 101 Goals Copying, emulating mentors, great people, heroes and heroines Re-exploring principles and values	Visual Thinking
6	Differentiating yourself Discovering Creative Style and Personality Type Examining Personal risk factor, risk-taking Moving forward B+ Vision Finalizing Personal Mission Statement Developing personal Concept of Operations Clarifying Strategies for Change (3-Sigma)	Different Thinking Lateral Thinking
7	Finishing 101 Goals & dreams (A-) Final touches on personal Vision (A-) Critical Success Factors for Change strategies for Change Plan for Action	Imaginative Thinking

THINKING ABOUT THINKING
Level 6 Change

Lateral Thinking

lat·er·al think·ing (lĭt″ōr-ŏl thĭng″kĭng)
Adj. 1. Of, relating to, or situated at or on the side. 2. Shifting perspective so as to view or consider something from another direction, including backwards.

ME, INC.®

As you read through this book, at the end of each chapter, I gave you some Me, Inc. work to do that corresponded with the thinking and mindshifts at that level of change. It involved thinking different and thinking about your own thinking, and then writing your thoughts down. I suggest that you use Blue Slips for your Me, Inc. idea-finding work because they keep you away from making lists, and that means that you can play around with your thoughts more, shuffle them around, and connect them in new and different ways. I would also suggest that you use Mindmapping in parallel with the Blue Slips; its an ideal way to get started on the process because its format allows you to easily add and refine your Me, Inc. as it evolves.

Mindmapping links and connects everything about you into an integrated big picture. As you explore and discover more and more of who you are and who you wish to become, you simply add those discoveries and insights to your Mindmap.

LEVEL 1 ME, INC.®
FOCUSED THINKING: THE RIGHT STUFF

You begin the process of Me, Inc. at Level 1 with some easy introspection—by first reflecting on yourself and some of the basic qualities that you have. Take inventory by thinking about your strengths and skills and abilities, knowledge you have, and perhaps some of the special things you know. Things that make you able to do what you do. Write twenty-five to thirty separate Blue Slips, or make a list—at least one full page.

A powerful exercise is to think of compliments people have given you on how you've done things or abilities they feel that you have, and, finally, things you are proud of having accomplished. What were some more unique or unusual skills and abilities and strengths that made it possible for you to do those things? Add them to your list. These are some of the basic things that make you what you are today.

182

LEVEL 2 ME, INC.®
THINKING ABOUT THINGS I REALLY DO RIGHT

Your initial Me, Inc.® work at Level 2 is not about efficiency, its rather about the underlying concept of Level 2: Doing the right things right. Thinking at Level 2 helps you more clearly define and amplify your collection of strengths and skills. Think about what you do well, what you are best at, what you often do better than those around you; think about major successes you've had, and some of your big accomplishments—the right things that you really do right.

Think back again about compliments people have paid you. Consider the basic qualities you have that helped you do the things they complimented you on—and focus on the way you did them, the how—right things you did right.

Now, shift your thinking and move up from the details of your skills, strengths, successes, and accomplishments to get a broader picture of yourself. With all those in mind, explore your purpose in life—what your focus seems to be. What do the abilities, skills and strengths you've developed, and your successes and accomplishments seem to highlight? Where and how does it look like you've been applying your strengths and skills and abilities? For right now, broadly consider this to be your "purpose"—your mission.

Capture that concept by writing on a Blue Slip "My purpose is…" and finish the sentence. Make a rough cut at it (about a B+), and write it in such a way that you leave plenty of room to play around with it—so you can change and refine your purpose as you progress through the Me, Inc.® process. You'll be coming back to it later to do some more thinking about it.

With your purpose roughed out, now use it to define your basic mission. Make a similar rough, B+ cut at your mission on a Blue Slip so it too can be played with and refined. Open up a major new leg on your Mindmap and label it "MY MISSION." (I usually arch mine out from the center and up into the top left-hand area of the paper. Later on I add my work on my vision higher up the leg, right in the corner area, which keeps my mission and my vision thinking strongly connected.) Add your

Level 6 Thinking

Change HOW You Think

· Think about the way you think
· Shift your perceptions
· Look at things differently
· Follow your intuition
· Force connections
· Be different
     ...lateral thinking

main ideas from your purpose and mission Blue Slips to this leg as branches coming off of it.

LEVEL 3 ME, INC.®
POSITIVE THINKING
AREAS TO IMPROVE, THINGS TO DO BETTER

Coming up with some goals to play with is your next step toward mentally incorporating. Goal setting begins as a Level 3 task—coming up with changes aimed at improving yourself. In the School for Innovators we have developed an exercise called "101 Goals" for kick-starting the Me, Inc.® process. This involves writing down 101 goals and "wishes" in one sitting before going to sleep! And it turns out to be a real stretch for most people.

Coming up with twenty to thirty goals, about one full page of notepaper, isn't difficult. These are the normal, everyday kinds of goals most people have and things you've always "wished" you do or accomplish.

With Level 3 positive thinking our thoughts frequently turn back to successes we've had, positive changes that happened as a result of something we did. Such thinking in turn can lead us back into thinking about the skills and abilities and strengths that enabled us to achieve such successes, as well as to the idea of improving them, making them even better. Similarly, we may find ourselves also recalling events that weren't successes because of some mistake we made, or a weakness. These present special areas to look at and explore possible changes to make to improve ourselves, to make those weaknesses better—and to come up with additional goals and wishes.

Which is great, because to push on up from thirty or so goals, to fifty to sixty—two pages worth—is much more challenging and is where most people get stuck. That's the point where they've reached the 1-Sigma boundary of "normal" thinking. So many of the goals and wishes we come up with at this stage focus on improving existing abilities and strengths, or developing new skills and capabilities to overcome weak spots. You may want to flag these a bit differently on your Mindmap.

184

Just as you used your successes and accomplishments to begin exploring your purpose, your goals and wishes can be used as a jumping-off point to explore another key aspect of Me, Inc.®—your basic values. If you back off and look at your wishes and goals, what is underlying them? What patterns of thinking can you discern? What appears to be important to you? Come up with six to eight life values, each on a separate Blue Slip, as a starter list and add another main leg titled "MY VALUES" to your Mindmap. As with the work you did on your purpose, this is a first cut that you'll come back to and do more work on later.

Now, given your goals and wishes, some of your key successes and accomplishments, and the basic values that you believe in strongly, what seem to be your operating principles? That is, how do you reflect those basic values in the way in which you live your life, in what you do? When you look at your accomplishments and successes, what do they seem to tell you about your operating principles? What principles and beliefs and values came into play with them? Try to come up with a short list of six to eight principles (B+) that you seem to be using in governing the manner in which you live your life—how you make decisions or choices, and how you come to conclusions. Write each principle on a separate Blue Slip and add them to another new leg on your Mindmap entitled "PRINCIPLES."

Given your goals, the basic values you believe in strongly, and how you carry out your life—your operating principles, it's now a good time to go back and take another look at your purpose. Rephrase your first cut somewhat—try to draw in some of your thoughts from your Level 3 thinking and add them to the PURPOSE area on your Mindmap.

With your Mindmap capturing all your Me, Inc. work, by now you've started to create a pretty interesting picture of who you are and where you're heading: abilities, accomplishments, beliefs, mission, principles, purpose, skills, strengths, successes, values. You've also done most of the normal, 1-Sigma thinking that forms the baseline for Me, Inc.®

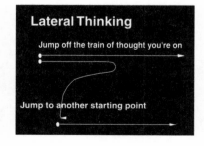

Lateral Thinking

Jump off the train of thought you're on

Jump to another starting point

LEVEL 4 ME, INC.®
REFOCUSED THINKING
THINGS TO CUT OUT OR STOP DOING.

Up to this point, moving through Levels 1, 2, and especially 3, you've pretty much focused on the positives in your life. Now, refocus your thinking and shift from the positive to the negative. Add a new subleg to your Mindmap labeled "Cut Out" and very rapidly write down as many things as you can think of that you want to cut out of your life, get off your agenda, or stop doing—stuff that's cluttering up what you want to do. Add some "bad" habits that you'd like to break, stop doing—that you don't want to have with you in your new Me, Inc.®

With refocused Level 4 thinking, its pretty natural to transition into rethinking everything: relook, review, reconsider, reexamine, reform, redecide, reengineer, re-create, reinvent, redo, rewrite, reverse, reexplore, rediscover, reorganize. And with all the Me, Inc.® information you've pulled together so far, this is a good time to reflect on and rewrite your first-cut mission statement. Rethink it now several times on new Blue Slips, paraphrase it—and use your insights to move to a higher level of change, rethinking everything you've worked on thus far. That should also spark you to rethink your goals and wishes.

When you move past the fifty to sixty goals point, the next wall you're likely to discover is at about eighty to eighty-five goals. An approach to take here is to switch "wouldn't it be great if" thinking and try some Level 4 thinking (doing away with things and habits) and Level 5 thinking (copying—doing things other people are doing). That shift will transition you into 2-Sigma—interesting thinking and interesting ideas, non-normal stuff.

LEVEL 5 ME, INC.®
COPYING AND ADAPTING THINGS
EXPLORING VALUES—YOUR HIGHER THINKING

The process of Me, Inc. up to this point has been predominantly inward focused. You've looked at the right things about you—- strengths, skills, abilities; you've looked at things you do right, in fact, the things you do very well as reflected in—successes and

186

accomplishments; and you've looked at things you might want to improve, and things to stop doing, habits to change.

With your Level 5 Me, Inc.® work, you begin to look outward. Start by adding a leg somewhere on your Mindmap with the names of people you admire or who have influenced you, your parents or relatives, teachers—"Great People" is a good title to give it. Consider some of the things you've seen them do or some of their major achievements. Reflect on some of their skills and abilities, on some of the ways they have proceeded through life, and see if they spark you to some higher levels of goals and wishes to add to your Mindmap. Who are your personal heroes and heroines? What is it that makes them special to you? Are there things they've done that you might copy and adapt to fit you? Add them to your 101 goals.

> *"You can really see a lot by observing."*
> *- Yogi Berra*

Benchmarking is the process of observing: identifying and studying specific processes, methods, and operations that the best of the best are doing and that really set the standard for everyone else or for a particular industry. Benchmarking goes beyond just observing, however—the second step is to copy and adapt those best practices to fit you and your operations—and in this case, that's your Me, Inc.® What and whom could you benchmark? Add these thoughts to your 101 goals as well.

A big piece of your Level 5 work involves looking both outward and inward as you identify and clarify your own principles and beliefs. They've been influenced strongly by the environment you grew up in and major figures and people in your life. You watch and observe and notice other people and develop your belief system and operating principles through that process.

Your principles and beliefs are a system of drivers behind how you govern your life—how you operate, how you make judgments and decisions. And they don't change much. Take another look at the principles and beliefs you wrote down earlier. Have

THINKING ABOUT THINKING

Diffferent Thinking
· **Rethink yourself**
 – Get in the habit of changing your habits
 – Redecide things regularly
 – Shift perspectives and perceptions

- LEVEL 6 THINKING

any of those principles and beliefs changed or shifted over time? How? Have some proven to hold solid over time? Have others fallen away? In the last few years have you changed how you operate? In pondering these questions you may get some deeper insights into who you are, what you believe, and who you seem to be becoming. If so, write them down, capture them on your Mindmap as well.

As you mentally incorporate, are there any particular principles, beliefs, or values that are aspirant values and principles for you—that is, they're things you would really want to aspire to, integrate into, and see reflected in your Me, Inc.®? Perhaps there are some things about your heroes or heroines or mentors and coaches that you'd like to adapt. If there are, don't treat them as goals of wishes, treat them as if they are already your values and principles, add them to the MISSION & VISION area of your Mindmap—make them start to become part of you right now.

LEVEL 6 ME, INC.®
LATERAL THINKING
UNIQUE AND DIFFERENT THINGS ABOUT YOU

Your work at Level 6 is to differentiate yourself, to explore everything you've done so far from a different perspective with a focus on different. Look over your Mindmap—what are the unique aspects of your Me, Inc.®? Add a new leg to your Mindmap labeled "Diffferent" and capture on it all the characteristics and things about you that are unusual and different— uniquely YOU. This Diffferent leg can be a powerful lever on which you can pull to catapult your thinking, your vision, and your mission into 3-Sigma.

Your creative thinking style and your personality type are a very unique aspect of you. The Kirton Adaption Innovation (KAI) Inventory and the Myers-Briggs Type Indicator (MBTI), mentioned several places in the book, give you a wealth of information and feedback about yourself that highlights both how you are similar to many people as well as how and where you are different. If you have any MBTI or KAI feedback information, add it to the "Diffferent" area on your mindmap.

188

How far did you get towards creating a list of 101 goals while reading the book? If you didn't finish (or even if you did!), now's the time to really push out, leveraging off the new 3-Sigma thinking you've been doing here at Level 6. The final stretch on your 101 goals list moves into the area of impossible dreams, into things you could never really see yourself doing but would love to somehow be able to. These last fifteen to twenty goals really do become out-of-the-box wishes that, for the person writing them down, are pure 3-Sigma different and impossible thinking. And later...they often become the seeds of greatness in your personal vision.

With your vision, purpose, values, principles, and goals now pretty clearly defined, the challenge becomes how to turn them all into an integrated, connected reality—how to make it all happen. This is about your mission, which draws everything together and focuses you for forward motion into the near-term aspects of making your Me, Inc.® come alive. Your mission, much like your vision, is uniquely you. It applies to you and to you only—your vision, your character, your purpose and goals—your differentness. Your vision and mission are pure Level 6.

Your values, principles, strengths, skills, and beliefs all combine powerfully to support you in carrying out your mission—and now is the time to finalize it, to rethink and rewrite it for the last time. Go back and finalize it. Like your vision, work at keeping your personal mission statement short—something that you can easily hold in your mind. Rephrase it on a Blue Slip—boil it down to its essence. Play with it, get a feel for it. Try it out—practice saying it aloud.

What's your mission? Most of the time, you'll find that your mission is unique. It applies to you and your unique vision, situation, business, and differentness—and your purpose. Your values, principles, strengths, and beliefs all add up to support you in carrying out your mission. Go back and finalize your mission now. Keep it to one short sentence. Whittle it down to its essence. Practice saying it out loud.

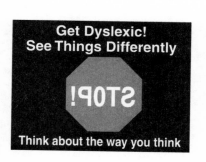

*"The more you're like yourself, the less
you're like somebody else."*
Source unknown

LEVEL 7 ME, INC.®
IMPOSSIBLE THINKING
YOUR VISION: WHAT IT IS YOU WANT TO BE

By going through this process of mental incorporation, you can
emerge with a new attitude towards change. Mentally incorporating yourself changes your thinking about yourself. Now you
can aim toward the future—your vision of yourself.

Think of the impossible. Push the envelope and stretch. Make
a wish. Make more. What do you want to become in ten or
twenty years? Now, write it down as a first step to getting there.

Now, try to sketch out a personal vision of the future, your
future, five to ten years from now. Describe it: What will you be
doing, what will have happened? How will your values and principles have played into that future? What will have changed?

With your vision, mission, values, principles, and goals clearly
defined, the challenge becomes how to make them all an integrated, connected reality—how to make it all happen. There are
a number of underpinning elements, things that must be in
place, that will be absolutely critical if you are to succeed. These
are your Critical Success Factors (CSFs)—things that either must
be or need to be in place for you to succeed with your mission,
vision, and purpose. There should be no more than eight total
(without the word "and" in any of them) and each should contain either the word "must" or "need" to be complete. Paired
Comparison Analysis (PCA) is an excellent tool to use to think
your CSFs through.

Finally, consider some broad strategies to follow in carrying
out your mission, for accomplishing your goals, for leveraging
and applying your strengths, values, and principles to move you
toward your vision.

190

THE ME, INC.® BUSINESS CARD

Now that you've gone through the entire Me, Inc.® process, look back over your work, particularly your Mindmap, and edit, condense, and refine. Focus down in each area of the Mindmap and identify those things that really connect with you—that really capture the essence of you as Me, Inc.® On the last page of this book is a special front-to-back Me, Inc.® form which you can cut out and fill in with the essentials of your Me, Inc.® work. It folds up to the size of a business card. Carry it with your normal business cards in your wallet, billfold, or purse, and get in the habit of regularly taking it out and using it as a reminder to refocus and remotivate yourself—or to explain just exactly who you are to someone.

Me, Inc.® involves a lot of thinking about thinking—backing off from where your head is now, quieting your mind, overview thinking, perspective thinking, exploratory thinking, discovery thinking—and a clear mind. Me, Inc.® is about strategic personal change—big change—and very different results. Oootching... starting with easy things to think about: things that you just do naturally to get normal results. Things that you don't really think about—thinking about the skills and knowledge and abilities and strengths that enable you to do them.

Deeper Insights
TIP!
- Reverse your thoughts...sthguoht
- not your ideas = idea
- Put 90⁰ turns on your ideas
- Turn your ideas inside out

APPENDIX II

The primary objectives of the School for Innovators are to:
- Educate and train students in the theory and practice of creative thinking and creative problem solving
- Inspire graduates to create environments for innovation, creativity, and positive change across their organizations
- Build and energize a network of highly motivated and demonstrably skilled guides and change agents

WHY A SCHOOL FOR INNOVATORS?

The concept behind the School for Innovators is to create a network of in-house leaders dedicated to creating an environment for innovation, creativity, continuous improvement, and positive change.

The school focuses on applying creativity to real problems within the environment of your own organization. Ample time is spent in "hands-on" mode learning and practicing new skills.

The goal of the school is faster, more effective translation of creative ideas into innovative solutions and bottom-line results to accelerate the pace of change.

WHAT?

The School for Innovators was conceived and has been developed through the process of customer-driven, continuous innovation: Students, graduates, and sponsoring organizations provide a continuous flow of ideas for virtually real-time incorporation in the curriculum.

The Estes Park, Colorado, Thinking Expedition format follows a particularly intense eight-day curriculum. The planned route integrates traditional small and large group facilitation tools with leadership skills, building on outdoors experiential learning.

The school is intended to provide the student with a basic understanding and perspective of the concepts, terminology, processes, and techniques associated with implementing innovation in large organizations. Supports for and barriers to innovation and creativity are explored, with emphasis on the issues and challenges around change, particularly large-scale change.

The linkage between thinking, ideas, creativity, invention, and innovation are examined, and Creative Problem Solving (CPS) models and techniques are covered in depth. Coupled with activity-based learning, the school is run on the model of an exciting and challenging expedition.

Graduates of the school will be able to immediately apply and integrate the material, general concepts, processes, and techniques learned into both personal

192

challenges and business world applications. In particular, the graduate will be able to appreciate the application of creative thinking skills and models to a wide range of situations and to assist small groups in the development of ideas and action plans.

STUDENTS MASTER . . .

- **Stand-up Facilitation.** Become comfortable with and skilled at the facilitation of small groups and meetings: Standing up and leading a group through an idea-generating session.
- **Creativity Techniques.** Learn how to use a variety of techniques to generate more creativity in yourself and your organization, how to move people toward thinking and looking at things differently.
- **Creative Style.** Take stock of your strengths, weaknesses, and particular style of looking at a problem—and similarly, learn how to compare and leverage creative styles within small and large groups. Learn how to THINK—better, differently, and more creatively. Learn when and how to diverge and when and how to converge in the creative problem-solving process.
- **Thinking about Thinking.** In connection with understanding your own creative style and risk orientation, you'll continuously be thinking about the way you think—as well as the way you don't think and how to move around and over your own mental blocks, filters, and paradigms (ShiftThink).
- **Colorado Mountain School.** Learn how to transfer and integrate creative thinking challenges and experiences outdoors into leading small groups and facilitating team building. Discover how Learning the Ropes and rock climbing can sharpen your own edge and push your risk-taking boundaries, teaching you how to think faster on your feet at every level of change and challenge. Then apply these skills to facilitating small groups and teams.
- **Creative Problem Solving (CPS).** Move from simple creative tools and techniques to your own model for facilitating all stages of Creative Problem Solving: Mess

THINKING ABOUT THINKING

How should we do things differently tomorrow?

Finding, Problem Finding, Data Finding, Idea Finding, Solution Finding, Acceptance Finding, and Action Planning.

- **Different Meetings.** Be able to plan, coordinate, and facilitate any meeting or conference so that its agenda is energized with innovative thinking and action. Learn how to refocus (on the spot) any meeting toward creative solutions and action planning.
- **Jump-Starting and Energizing Ideas.** Learn how to rapidly expand and develop an idea into an overall concept built around a creative implementation action plan. Learn how to move an idea to social acceptance, how to build a network of support for an idea, and how to launch it.
- **Lateral Thinking Excursions.** Learn how to lead a group into new thinking directions with visual connection techniques and the use of video clips as springboards. Advanced facilitation processes involving pictures and color are used to get groups "unstuck" on the really tough problems by tapping their hidden Picasso/artistic side in excursions away from the obvious.
- **The 7 Levels of Change.** Become fully comfortable with how to use the seven basic levels of change as a model for connecting Creativity and Innovation with Continuous Improvement and Quality. Learn how to facilitate the change process across the spectrum from Level 1 (Doing the Right Things) to breakthrough thinking at Level 7 (Doing Things That Can't Be Done).
- **Hands-on-Idea Approach.** Get direct experience and hands-on practice with new techniques and tools during the school by working with real clients on tough, real-world issues and problems.
- **Innovator's Toolbox.** Leave the school with a Creative Thinking Journal and tool kit full of ideas and techniques for facilitating change at every level of the Quality and Innovation processes.

WHO?—AND WHAT?

Normally limited to twenty-four participants, students in the school are backed by sponsors who help set the focus for the curriculum, and who commit to championing the

194

graduates as intrapreneurs and change agents in their organizations. Students bring real-world problems and develop strategies for innovation in their own work environments.

Armed with different creative problem-solving skills, problem-solving techniques, and their own creative enthusiasm, graduates are able to return and proactively infuse innovation into every aspect of their own organizations (management meetings, planning sessions, issue resolution, and conferences) to significantly accelerate the pace of change.

WHEN?— AND WHERE?
Estes Park, Colorado. Starts Saturday, 9:00 A.M. or 2:00 P.M., and ends the following Saturday at 9:00 P.M. in April/May and September. Other dates in different locations can be booked by special arrangement for corporate groups.

ALUMNI
The School for Innovators' students have come from a wide range of organizations: Exxon, IBM, Proctor & Gamble, Johnson & Johnson, Kentucky Fried Chicken (Australia and New Zealand), Ford Motor Company, E-Systems, Chase Manhattan Bank, Texaco, the National Security Agency, U.S. Navy, Inroads, R. J. Reynolds, Hoechst Celanese Corporation. School for Innovators graduates are making change happen worldwide in some very "different" ways.

BEFORE GOING ON EXPEDITION
The School for Innovators operates like an expedition. A Thinking Expedition is different. Often people who want to go on expedition don't realize just how different things will be.

Every Thinking Expedition is different. The route is unclear, and little is known about it. Frequently what is planned does not work out. The results of a Thinking Expedition are unpredictable. Much of what happens is beyond the guide's control.

A Thinking Expedition is built on trust. Your normal routine will change radically. You'll be working long hours with little

3 - Sigma Change

Diffferent-Doing things no one else is doing
Impossible-Doing things that can't be done

rest or sleep. Meals and breaks are taken when the operation permits. You are sometimes going to feel very uncomfortable.

A Thinking Expedition is not a meeting or training session. You will be expected to be a full team member. You may have to pitch in and work extra hard to make things happen. You may miss the summit because of helping a team member down safely. The team member needing help could be you.

Going on expedition is a big commitment.

Level 7 Change

Doing Things
That Can't Be Done

HOW TO CREATE A
7 LEVELS OF CHANGE
PRESENTATION OR WORKSHOP

THE SLIDE SHOW

The "Slide Show"—the set of 35 mm slides at the bottom of the pages in the book —was how I developed the concept of the 7 Levels of Change. They are high quality multi-color slides, designed and produced by a Graphics artisan, to carry the presentation and ideas of the 7 Levels of Change in the most powerful way I could come up with. It was not until quite some time after I had been using the slides in presentations and workshops that I began to write up some of the key ideas behind the 7 Levels of Change.

GETTING STARTED: ONE GOOD SLIDE

Similarly, I didn't develop the 7 Levels of Change overnight. I started with one slide that had three levels on it. It was part of a training workshop on continuous improvement and innovation. At some point the slide changed to five levels, and then to six with the heading "Levels of Innovation." I played around with that concept a lot and one day the slide added another level and the heading changed to "Levels of Change." I used each one of those slides for quite a while, dropping it into 35 mm slide presentations and talks and workshops I was giving on innovation, creativity and out-of-the-box thinking. Just one good slide.

You can give a whole talk or lecture around one point, around one picture, around one good slide.

As you become comfortable with that one good slide, you can add to it, expand on it by putting a few more slides behind it—maybe one more good slide, such as a quote you like to close your presentation with, or a picture that you can really talk about. Flip back and take a look at the picture of Amy and me climbing the Twin Owls in Estes Park. That's a picture of Level 7 Change—the impossible—doing something that can't be done.

TAKING THE SLIDE SHOW APART

The sequence that the slides at the bottom of the pages are in is a standard presentation flow I've used very successfully for some time. It should also work for you

198

in that order. However, there are really several different but related concepts in the set of slides:

THE BASIC MODEL OF THE 7 LEVELS OF CHANGE

The Mindshift Model: Different results (Do things different (Think Diffferent (Think about Thinking The 7 Levels of Thinking that correspond to each of the 7 Levels of Change (doing).

Take the Slide Show apart. Find the basic 7 Levels of Change slide—the one that has all 7 Levels of Change on it. That's your "one good slide" to start with.

Next, notice that each Level of Change has a "header" slide that breaks it out as a separate section—essentially the "one-liners" on your "one good slide." Put them in behind your one good slide and you have an eight-slide outline-style presentation. If you now come up with an example or a story about a specific change that has been made at each level of change, you have a presentation. To dress it up a bit, you may want to "frame it" with the slide that just has the word "CHANGE" on it and use that to open your talk. To close your talk, you might use the Einstein quote or the slide that defines results as "a measurable success" to make the point that each Level of Change is about "doing" something—and when you do something, you get results.

You now have about a ten-slide presentation.

To put a little life into it, all you need are seven good snapshots of people you know or work with involved in the 7 Levels of Change. Cut out the front-to-back card in the back of the book that has examples for each level of change at both work and at home. Use the card to cue you for snapshot opportunities: People being effective—doing the right things; being efficient—doing things right; improving things—doing things better; getting rid of waste—stopping doing things; doing things no one else is doing—diffferent; and doing something that can't be done—the impossible. Try it at home with your family tonight—get them to help you put together your presentation by taking their pictures doing some of the things on the cue card. Bring in your camera to work tomorrow, tell people they're going to be in your presentation, and take their picture while they're actually engaged in a particular level of change. Get them to tell you about it—then you've got seven good stories to go with your seven good slides.

Tip! Tell Personal Stories

Share real things, facts, and experiences about you. People communicate via stories. If I begin to tell you a story, you will immediately begin to search for a story in your memory that will "connect" or reinforce mine with a similar experience of your own. These stories powerfully reinforce the personal slides (e.g., family, children, friends, coworkers) in your presentation.

You now have a seventeen-slide presentation.

If you only talk for sixty to ninety seconds about each level of change, with a little bit of time at the opening and close, you have a ten-minute presentation. If you get into it a bit, and go for two minutes about the example at each level, telling some of the story behind the snapshot, you have a very snappy and interesting fifteen-minute presentation that people will remember.

Tip! Take Snapshots

Snapshots are a poor man's answer to professionally prepared slides. Buy a 35 mm PhD camera (Push here, Dummy!) with built-in flash, carry it everywhere with you, keep it loaded with slide film, and carry an extra roll of film.

Collect ideas with your camera. Shoot anything that you could talk about. Start to seriously take snapshots and photos. Notice signs and posters (photograph them). Take pictures of magazine covers, newspaper headlines.

Buy slides. Check out souvenir shops, museum sales shops. The slide sets they sell have been shot professionally, great shots of famous things, and they're going to be better than any you can ever take, no matter how good you are, plus they're ready to use now.

200

You can also make your own "poor boy" text slides by simply writing on flip charts, or using blue poster board with white press-letters, and then taking a 35 mm slide snapshot of that.

Tip! Get a Few Good "Quotes"

Start collecting good quotes (ones you like) that support what you're talking about. People love them and they essentially bring a "second speaker" up front to support you. Put them in a word processor document or on 3x5 cards where you can go review them for "connections" to what you're going to talk about. Start carrying them in your mental hip pocket—get comfortable with them. Practice using them in conversations—if necessary, at the dinner table with your family until everyone knows them. Then they'll roll off your tongue.

Every time you get a few queued up, have them made into 35 mm slides. Then, get focused: Come up with seven good quotes, one that you're comfortable using with each level of change.

You now have twenty-four personalized 35 mm slides added into your presentation, and you may now be pushing about a twenty-minute talk.

WHY 35 MM SLIDES?

They work. A large percentage of people are visual learners, some eighty to eighty-five percent. Like newscasters sound bites, 35 mm slides are "eye bites"—they grab and hold your mind, reinforcing or expanding the point you want to make. 35 mm slides give you more control and more professional "aura" than any single technique or tool, even if you're only using a handful. People intuitively understand (i.e., "think") that designing, producing the slides, and organizing them into a slide tray takes some work. Further, they realize that there is a very set sequence they're going to move through (not like overheads, which can be shuffled around).

THINKING ABOUT THINKING
Level 7 Change
Breakthrough Thinking
break·through think·ing (br≥k"thrö" th∧ng"k∧ng) n. 1. The act of overcoming or penetrating an obstacle or restriction through the formation of a mental image of something that is neither perceived as real nor present to the senses. 2. Thought which leads to a major achievement or success that permits further progress, as in technology.

When you punch the forward button on a slide projector, you immediately re-take control and refocus the group back on the screen.

Also notice that you haven't written a script in this process. The slides are your script—you simply explain the point that the slides highlight or tell the story behind them. Simple, but not simplistic.

NOTE! 35 mm slides are not expensive (but people think they are!)—you can have a custom-made slide produced for as little as five dollars. Optima Image (Robin Dallred) in Houston has a first-class operation. Robin does the input and design work for you and produces what you want—satisfaction guaranteed. You can rough out a slide you've just discovered you need (while you're flying to a conference), call him when you land, and he'll overnight it to you... and they'll match the format you've been using (such as these in my Slide Show).

Call Optima Image at (713) 977-8424.

MAKING YOUR SLIDE SHOW DIFFERENT

Using Your Slide Show
Three "how to talk slides" tips:

Never read everything on a slide to a group. They can read a lot faster than you can talk.

On a text slide, start reading it from the bottom up. People automatically start reading from the top down. By the time they unconsciously shift to where you are on the slide, they will have read the top half, you will have read the bottom, and you can pop to the next slide—moving things along very rapidly.

As soon as the next slide comes up, verbally connect it with one of the previous two slides. If you habitually try to do this, even if you don't do it more than 50 percent of the time, your slides will really "flow" as a sequence.

202

Tip! Involvement and interaction

Get people involved in your talk fast—immediately! "Connect" them as quickly as you can. Make your audience DO something. Make them think about something they've personally been involved in that connects to your talk—a personal example. Show a photo of yourself doing something, involved in some particular level of change, and then ask them for a similar example.

Use the tools and techniques I've explained in the book at each level of change. Ask them a question. Make them write something down as an answer or an "idea"—and then make them pair up and talk to the person next to them about it. Get them sharing experiences or ideas relative to your subject.

Tip! Give them time to think and write

forty-five seconds to one minute, and time it with your watch. DON'T cut them off short. Watch the audience for energy level. Doing any of this is different and they'll need time to oootch into it.

Tip! Write It Down! (Blue Slips)

Blue Slips are a diffferent, inexpensive, simple way to get people involved and interacting with you. Add a small "module" early on (J.I.T.—right before you use the tool) that explains what Blue Slips are, how they work, and then use them. Make your audience write a few ideas down. Insert it in Level 1 Change as an example of "Doing the Right Things" and then reinforce the rules of Blue slipping in Level 2 Change as an example of "Doing things right."

As you finish explaining each level of change, ask everyone to write down one idea they have for implementing a change at that level; when the presentation is over, each person will have a set of seven ideas that they can take away with them

Use "pairing and sharing" to get even more involvement going—ask people to pair up and discuss the Blue Slip idea(s) they've just written down in response to your question with

THINKING ABOUT THINKING

Breakthrough

Doing something so different that it cannot be compared with any existing practices or perceptions.

the person sitting next to them. This reinforces their idea, and the audience really comes alive. You can ask for "feedback"—what are some of the ideas or thinking the pairs have come up with? You can also use it as an example of Level 3 Change—building on and improving an idea.

You can collect some of the Blue Slip ideas at the end of the session to give you insights into how things registered. Take that a step further and "storyboard" those you collect, word-process them into a summary, and give or mail that back to everyone who was in your talk or presentation. NOTE: This is work! However, nobody else does this so it really differentiates you and really adds value to your participants in terms of fast feedback.

Note: 3x5 cards are also a form of "Blue Slips" and are always available, are easy to get, and can be used—and people know how to write on them! Just don't tell me about it—I feel that it bastardizes the diffferent aspect of Blue Slips. If no Blue Slips and no 3x5 cards are available (e.g., at an after-dinner talk), get them to write on their napkins or tear up sheets of paper into small Blue Slip-sized pieces. That's both diff*ferent* and dramatic.

Tip! Today's Newspaper

If you can't find an article, line, or quote in the morning newspaper that relates to whatever it is you are going to talk about on a given day, you haven't looked. Buy (or get delivered to your room if in a hotel) all the newspapers available. Scan headlines fast—don't read, you're not looking for news, you're looking for resonance with YOUR topic, your key words.

Carry the newspaper in to the talk with you, put it on the podium (or even better, on your "stuff" table), and pick it up once or twice to read the headline or quote(s) to the group. This creates a very powerful picture of timeliness, currency, importance, and an amazing aura of "Wow!" around you as a person who would even spot that in a paper when the majority of the people in the room haven't even read a newspaper that day. Using a newspaper like that falls in the category of "stuff."

204

Tip! "Stuff"

"Stuff" is physical. "Stuff" is things you can pick up, turn around, look at, feel. "Stuff" is pieces of things, old things, personal things. Memorabilia. Photographs. Collect any and all "stuff" that you think you might somehow possibly use during the talk as props, supports, or background, or that are something you could just have fun with—things that you could use to demonstrate or reinforce a specific level of change. Check your purse or wallet, particularly just before you talk—they're always full of interesting "stuff" you can use to personalize your points.

Start collecting "stuff" that oddly relates to each level of change. Notice, pick up, buy "stuff" that somehow represents some of the things that are important to you—symbolically maybe—or which somehow capture the essence or make a good metaphor for you. Keep all your "stuff" in a bag, box, or something that you can take with you to a talk, set on the table, and start pulling things out of.

Tip! "Mindmapping"—Planning your slide show.

Mindmap whatever you're going to talk about. Include any and all "stuff" you're going to use as props (Note: "Stuff" lends itself well to pictures/sketches on your Mindmap). Be sure to add in any "how" as well (e.g., "hold up Wheaties box" or "tell story about Leroy Johnson"). Mindmapping is one of the fastest and most effective ways to brainstorm with yourself. You can, with a little practice, literally explode onto a blank sheet of paper.

Use larger-than-normal paper (e.g., legal size, inside of a grocery bag, wrapping paper turned inside out). Why??? Because it's Level 6 Change—diffferent for you, and it will probably be different for your audience—AND you can use it during your talk as "stuff." You can hold it up, point to the Mindmap, and say"…okay—this is where I am right now—I'm talking about this…" (very effective, even though nobody can read what you're holding up—but it does show that you have a plan and that you clearly spent some unusual time thinking about what you're talking about).

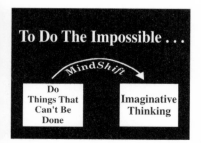

Tip! Just DO it!

1. Have one truly great, impactful "cover" slide made to open your talk—what people see at the start. Customize it so this 7 Levels of Change talk fits you, your company, your organization. You can talk about a cover slide, or talk with it behind you, for a long time. And you can put it back on at the end of the sequence to close and refocus the presentation.

2. Drop your "collection" of snapshots of real people behind your cover slide and just talk about what's happening in the picture. If you don't have a cover slide, start with as dramatic a photo as you can of your topic—a Level 7 change happening—it'll bring your talk alive!

3. Finally, use your "stuff"—it's really multimedia. Put it on a small table up front where you can easily grab, pick up and talk about. To get fancier, take some slide snapshots of your "stuff" and drop them in your slide show—they'll cue you to pick up your stuff and talk about it (e.g., shot of the Wheaties box sitting on the breakfast table, shot of the copy of *Fortune* magazine you're going to use laying open on your desk—real-life pictures!)

HOW TO ORDER THE 35 MM SLIDES IN THE BOOK

Tip! DON'T!

Think Level 5: Copy them instead. Make your own "poor boy" overhead transparencies from the examples in the book. While they won't be in color and they won't be as impressive as the 35 mm slides I use, they'll do fine to get you started.

The small slide images in the lower left-hand corner of the pages in the book are actual copies of most of the set of 35 mm color slides I use to lead workshops and give major presentations. They're the "framework" and "background" between which I sandwich in personal snapshots and other customized slides to flesh out the presentations I give.

I've developed a "Notes and Tips" booklet that provides an outline of key points for each slide and a script to use as well as tips on how to drop in your own personal slides and how

206

to tie all the slides together as the sequence you've created unfolds. I've organized the slides into three increasingly "complete" sets of slides that range from a framework to a basic set to an enhanced version.

THE FRAMEWORK SLIDES

A "framework" set of forty-five slides (a subset of the slides shown in the book)—four to six slides for each of the 7 Levels of Change. This set does not include many of the prefacing nor the concluding slides (the Mindshift Model, the thinking mindshifts corresponding to each level, and the diagram and graphics slides which end the sequence in the book). You might view this set as a Levels 1 & 2 change in what you're doing today—an effective and efficient step up from simply talking about the 7 Levels of Change to actually presenting a visual framework.

THE SLIDE SHOW

A basic set of eighty slides—the majority of the slides shown in the book. Some of these slides may not match those shown in the book exactly, since I may have upgraded or modified them through the continuous process of innovation and change on which the Slide Show is built. You might think of this set as making a Level 5 change—getting an "official copy" of most of the slides in this book which you can then adapt to whatever you're doing today.

THE DIFFFERENT SLIDE SHOW

This is an expanded set of 120 slides or more, essentially the Slide Show (the 80 slides described above), most of the remaining slides shown in the book, augmented further with a number of different slides that amplify each Level of Change—adding more detail and breadth (graphics, quotes, drawings, additional Blue Slip questions, tips, and tools).

Imagination

i·mag·i·na·tive think·ing (Ă-măj"Ō-nŌ-tĂv thĂng"kĂng) n. 1. The formation of a mental image of something that is neither perceived as real nor present to the senses. 2. The ability to confront and deal with reality by using the creative power of the mind. 3. Mental resourcefulness.

ORDERING 35 MM SLIDE SETS

For 1997–1998, the price for the Framework Slide Set of forty-five slides is $149.00, which includes shipping and handling (within the United States). Texas residents need to add 8.25 percent sales tax.

You may order the basic Framework Slide Set with a check or money order (made payable to: OSI, Inc.), and also additional information on the larger and enhanced sets of slides from:

The Office of Strategic Innovation, Inc.
10682 Beinhorn Road
Houston, Texas 77024

Or by E-mail through our web site:

7Levels@thinking-expedition.com

Level 7 Thinking

Imagine and Visualize
Mindshift your brain into high gear
- Imagine: Would'nt it be great if...
- Conjure up a miracle
- That's impossible!
- Get a little crazy
- Make 90^0 turns
- Breakout! *...imaginative thinking*

BIBLIOGRAPHY

Adaptors and Innovators. Michael Kirton (ed., 1994).
A collection of articles and papers centered around the Kirton Adaption-Innovation (KAI) Inventory. Chapter 1, "A Theory of Cognitive Style," by Michael Kirton himself, gives excellent insights into KAI, differentiates between creative style and creative level, and describes the characteristics and general profiles of adaptors and innovators. Chapter 4, "Adaptors and Innovators at Work," also written by Kirton, provides some very useful details for practitioners using the KAI with groups and teams dealing with change. For me, in my work with small groups and teams, and particularly on problem-solving Thinking Expeditions, the KAI instrument and theory have proven to be one of our most powerful tools.

Brainpower. Karl Albrecht. Prentice Hall (1980).
This book, coupled with a short video by the same name and featuring John Houseman, profoundly impacted my approach to thinking and my thinking about thinking—and the development of *The School for Innovators* as a way to teach people how to think, be, and do different. Albrecht does a great job of establishing a vocabulary and conceptual baseline around the art and practice of thinking. It is also very much a J.I.T. book—one that can be opened anywhere, anytime, for any length of time, with a high return in value. Also has lots of pithy quotes.

Breakpoint and Beyond. George Land. Harper Business (1992).
Study of change in business and the cycles of business. Useful model built around interconnected S-curves and analogies with nature's cycles. Reinforced very strongly my own thinking about the relationships and connections between quality, continuous improvement, creativity, and innovation, and the model for *The 7 Levels of Change*.

Breakthrough Thinking. Gerald Nadler & Shozo Hibino (1990).
Excellent mix of western and eastern perspectives and thinking about thinking, particularly the creative problem-solving area. The authors describe seven principles around a systemic approach that can lead to breakout thinking and breakthrough results. I found both chapter 3 ("Pushing for Breakthrough") and chapter 5 ("The Purposes Principle")

valuable in looking at the higher levels of change as well as in understanding the corresponding shifts in thinking that must take place at every level of change in doing. Helpful model for clarifying the process of problem-expanding and problem-finding.

The Creative Attitude. Roger Schank.

Thinking by a leading researcher in artificial intelligence and expert systems development. Unusual insights into how creative people think, approach thought and ideas, how they store and retrieve data and information, and the role scripts and story-telling play in thinking. Good stuff about asking questions, problem approaching and problem framing.

The Character of Organizations. William Bridges (1992).

A definitive book that uses the Myers-Briggs Types to segue into similarly defining the character (type) of teams, groups, and organizations. Provides insight after insight into why different organizations act the way they do, how they view and deal with change, and why even lower levels of change are often difficult for them to handle. We have discovered a number of applications for Bridges's theory and the concepts of his Organizational Character Index (OCI) with Thinking Expedition teams; in fact, our discoveries in this area have led us to complement the KAI Inventory with the MBTI in virtually everything we do that relates to team bonding and work at higher levels of change (levels 5, 6, and 7) with groups.

Created in Japan. Sheridan Tatsumo (1990).

A very diffferent look at creativity, ideas, change, and innovation in Japan. Tatsumo moves through the 7 Levels of Change in his chronicling of Japan's transformation from imitator and improver (level 5, level 2, level 3 changes) to world-class innovator (level 6 and level 7 changes). In doing that, he brings out both the changes behind the changes in those shifts as well as the deliberate mindshifts and thinking about thinking that Japanese culture is going through. The influence of Zen as a baseline for diffferent thinking about thinking is interestingly touched on in the context of change.

Creative Education Foundation (CEF). Alex Osborne (1954).
The Creative Education Foundation (Buffalo, New York) is a nonprofit service-oriented organization comprised of hundreds of qualified and creative leaders who are dedicated to bringing the benefits of innovation, creativity, ideas, and problem solving to individuals and organizations. Dr. Alex Osborne, an innovative advertising executive (and the inventor of brainstorming, as we know it today), founded the CEF in 1954. Osborne wanted to make a difference in people's lives through creativity—thus, the mission of the foundation is to promote and develop creativity and innovation—which it does primarily through its annual Creative Problem Solving Institute, or CPSI (sip-see), as it's more commonly known. Call 1-800-447-2774 for information.

CPSI—The Creative Problem Solving Institute. Alex Osborne and Sidney Parnes (1955).
A very diffferent experience in thinking and doing! This intensive, action-packed, week-long institute is dedicated to helping groups and individuals develop their creativity and problem-solving skills. Launched in 1955, CPSI today has forty-plus years of creative thinking behind it. Typically, more than two hundred separate workshops, presentations, training sessions, and experiences are offered, and attendance runs near a thousand. There are several structured tracks to choose from and the Extending Program offers the option of tailoring the entire week to fit you and your interests. Many of the ideas, tools, techniques, and concepts connected with the 7 Levels of Change and the Thinking Expedition were developed and field-tested at CPSI. For me, CPSI is a continuous Wow!—a profound experience that has enriched and changed my life every year I've been there. This is a "must go to" for anyone interested in diffferent—diffferent thinking, diffferent doing, diffferent results. And . . . it's held in Buffalo, New York, every year toward the end of June, to add to the diffferent even more! Call the Creative Education Foundation (CEF), 1-800-447-2774 for detailed information on CPSI.

212

The Dead Poets Society. Touchstone Pictures (1989).
A profound movie about thinking different at every level of change. Actor Robin Williams, as poetry teacher John Keating at a boys' prep school, takes his students through increasingly higher levels of change and shifts in their thinking. The scene in which Keating has the class *Riippp!* out the whole introduction to their textbook is dramatic level 4 change (cutting—stopping doing things). And the famous scene in which he stands upon his desk in order to look at the world in a different way is pure level 6 change (difffferent: doing what no one else is doing). A must-see (at least twice!) for people who see themselves in roles as change agents.

DeBono's Thinking Course. Edward de Bono (1985).
A fairly "structured" approach to teaching thinking and teaching people to think differently. In each chapter, de Bono has a large number of exercises, processes, and approaches that are useful for anyone interested in "different" with regards to thinking. The basic concept of the book influenced me strongly in developing both *The School for Innovators and Think 101: How to Think Different.*

The Einstein Factor. Win Wenger and Richard Peo (1996).
This is a great book for anyone who's interested in the how-to's for mindshifting into thinking difffferent—and into greater levels of sharpness, insight, and overall intelligence. I have tied a number of the tools and techniques described by Win Wenger to specific levels of change. Although I did not include "Image Streaming" as a tool to use in connection with level 6 and level 7 thinking, I probably should have—it's powerful and it works. Tip—get a copy of this book and write in the margins!

Oh the Thinks You Can Think! Dr. Seuss. Random House (1975).
A fun book for the serious thinker, and a real classic on thinking. "Think left and think right, think low and think high, oh the thinks you can think if only you try." Level 6 stuff…if you think about it.

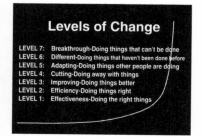

Levels of Change

LEVEL 7: Breakthrough-Doing things that can't be done
LEVEL 6: Different-Doing things that haven't been done before
LEVEL 5: Adapting-Doing things other people are doing
LEVEL 4: Cutting-Doing away with things
LEVEL 3: Improving-Doing things better
LEVEL 2: Efficiency-Doing things right
LEVEL 1: Effectiveness-Doing the right things

People Types and Tiger Stripes. Gordon Lawrence (1995).
This is the new and improved version of an already great
book on how to apply Myers–Briggs Type theory. Lawrence
has added six new chapters that significantly expand on the
book's applicability. The focus of the book is on identifying
mindsets, learning styles, teaching styles, motivation patterns—all of which are extremely useful for designing and
planning work to lead people into change—and learning is
a critical aspect of change. Gives especially useful insights
into teachers and teaching, a correspondingly key aspect of
leading change and change teams.

Please Understand Me. Robert Kiersy & Marilyn Bates
(1984).
A classic off the Myers–Briggs bookshelf. Easy to read and
follow, helps understand the how and the why of a wide
range of disconnects between different types. Includes an
abbreviated self-scoreable MBTI inventory that requires no
certification to use.

The Stuff Americans Are Made Of. Josh Hamond & James
Morrison (1996).
Very useful in thinking about why certain kinds of changes
are easy to make while others are much more difficult. The
authors define and describe seven cultural forces that drive
Americans in their thinking, doing, and changing. Chapter 2
("The Future is Now—American Time") really helps in
understanding how level 2 change and ideas (efficiency—
doing things right) connect so immediately with people; it
further highlights the value of the KAI's efficiency subscale
in small team idea finding. Chapter 4 ("The Impossible
Dream") provides some powerful insights into why Thinking
Expeditions work so well and how ootching teams to level 7
change and ideas (impossible—doing things that can't be
done) energizes them so amazingly.

Levels of Change

1-Sigma   **Continuous Improvement**
    Level 1
    Level 2
    Level 3
2-Sigma   **Process Reengineering**
    Level 4
    Level 5
3-Sigma   **Breakout and Breakthrough**
    Level 6
    Level 7

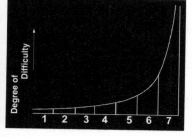

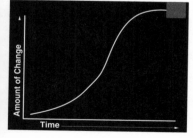

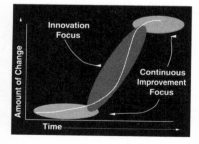

THE SEVEN LEVELS OF CHANGE
A STRATEGY FOR CREATIVITY, INNOVATION, AND CONTINUOUS IMPROVEMENT

 AT WORK...

LEVEL 1: DO THE RIGHT THINGS

- Set priorities
- Focus!
- Do what's important first
- Become more effective

LEVEL 2: DO THINGS RIGHT

- Follow procedures
- Understand standards
- Clean up your mess
- Become more efficient

LEVEL 3: DO THINGS BETTER

- Think about what you're doing
- Find ways to improve things
- Listen to suggestions
- Help, coach, and mentor others

LEVEL 4: DO AWAY WITH THINGS

- Ask "Why?"
- Use the 80:20 rule - Simplify
- Stop doing what doesn't count
- Refocus continuously

LEVEL 5: DO THINGS OTHER PEOPLE ARE DOING

- Notice and observe more
- Read about best practices
- Think before you think
- Copy!

LEVEL 6: DO THINGS THAT HAVEN'T BEEN DONE

- Think about thinking
- Ask "Why not?"
- Combine new technologies
- Focus on different, not similar

LEVEL 7: DO THINGS THAT CAN'T BE DONE

- Question assumptions
- Defocus: Get a little crazy
- Break the rules!
- What's impossible today, but...?
- Wouldn't it be amazing if . . ."
- Where will it take pure magic?

THE SEVEN LEVELS OF CHANGE
A STRATEGY FOR CREATIVITY, INNOVATION, AND CONTINUOUS IMPROVEMENT

AT HOME . . .

LEVEL 1 : DO THE RIGHT THINGS

- Talk and communicate
- Keep your promises
- Do your chores
- Start a savings program

LEVEL 2 : DO THINGS RIGHT

- Set family priorities for fun
- Start an investment plan
- Praise and compliment
- Actually listen

LEVEL 3 : DO THINGS BETTER

- Be more loving & supporting
- Become more cost conscious
- Develop new habits - grow
- Increase amount of savings

LEVEL 4 : DO AWAY WITH THINGS

- Stop impulse buying
- Stop negative 'self-talk'
- Eliminate blaming and criticizing
- Simplify your life
- Detoxify your life
- Turn off the lights

LEVEL 5 : DO THINGS OTHER PEOPLE ARE DOING

- Copy what works
- Stick ideas on the refrigerator
- Really take a vacation
- Read, study, discuss

LEVEL 6 : DO THINGS THAT HAVEN'T BEEN DONE

- Try something you've never tried
- Get professional help
- Incorporate → We, Inc.
- Go on a family adventure!

LEVEL 7 : DO THINGS THAT CAN'T BE DONE

- Dream the impossible dream
- "Wouldn't it be great if we...."
- Enjoy each other
- Make a dream come true

©1991 - THE OFFICE OF STRATEGIC INNOVATION, INC.
10682 BEINHORN ROAD - HOUSTON, TEXAS 77024
(713) 984-9611

My Principle and Critical Success Factors:

My Values:

My Real Strengths:

My Vision for Me, Inc.

My Mission as Me, Inc.

My Stratagies Are:

My Plan for Action ("I will… by…)